The 7 Deadly Retirement Sins

Ryan Zacharczyk, CFP®

THE 7 DEADLY RETIREMENT SINS
33 Retirees, 7 Lessons, 1 Life Changing Journey

Address all inquiries to:
Ryan Zacharczyk
RyanZ@7sinsbook.com

www.7sinsbook.com
www.zynergyretirement.com

ISBN: 978-1-938686-00-9
Library of Congress Control Number: 2012943525

Editor: Jody Calendar: Calendar Communications
Jacket and Cover Design: Shore Creative Group
Interior Book Design: Shore Creative Group

Every attempt has been made to properly source all quotes

Printed in the United States of America

FIRST EDITION

For additional copies visit:
www.7sinsbook.com

Should we all confess our sins to one another
we would all laugh at one another for
our lack of originality

- **Kahlil Gibran**

Part I : The Beginning

Chapter 1
I Am Sam

The challenging life of a freelance writer is not for the meek. It's a constant struggle that would threaten even the hardiest of souls. But a little more than two years ago, at 26 years old, this battle was my day-to-day reality. In fact, it would have been a leap to label myself a writer - it was my night job of waiting tables and tending bar that paid the bills. Writing was really more of a dream, my passion.

My name is Samantha Jane Clason and my background is far from extraordinary. I was born and raised in a small suburb of Albany, New York and went to the University of Albany, where I received my degree in communications with a less-than-stellar 2.6 GPA. After college I spent most of my time jumping from one crummy job to the next, hoping that just one of my many writing projects might pay the bills.

Now, however, I find myself a renowned expert in the area of retirement. How, you may be wondering, does my entirely average background qualify me for such a thing? It doesn't.

In fact, the thought of strangers coming up to me on the street and asking for advice about their retirement would have been laughable back then. Today, it is a regular occurrence. The contrast between then and now is remarkable. Two years ago I was renting a studio apartment in Red Bank, New Jersey above a music store called Jack's Music Shop. Their volume of business made the rent cheap and cheap rent is what I needed.

I had barely enough money to keep the creditors at bay each

month. Despite the fact that I borrowed only what I needed to survive, owing money to my friends and family was an uncomfortable but necessary part of life. My credit cards totaled a whopping $9,000, which often led to astronomical late fees and my debt continued to expand. I didn't even own a car, which was probably for the best because I couldn't afford it.

The realization that there was no end in sight kept me up many nights. I saw no escape from the financial quagmire I had created. The only lifeboat remaining on this sinking ship was an inheritance of $23,000 from when my father passed away. I left it untouched in bank CD's so I wouldn't be tempted to use the last remnants of my father's legacy to pay back MasterCard.

Make no mistake; despite the financial hardships, I was proud of myself for living my dream and I know my father would have been equally proud. Like so many before him, my Dad gave up his own dream - playing the saxophone professionally - to support his growing family. He begrudgingly took a job at my uncle's dingy garage and worked as a mechanic for the remainder of his days.

Dad sold out for financial comfort and wanted to protect his children from the same fate. I often felt that a part of him died with his dream, and his insistence that I live my passion stays close to my heart every day. I can only assume that if he had seen the size of the cockroaches I had in the kitchen back then, he might have altered his advice a bit. However, his words clung to me like a warm blanket on many cold nights.

But, that was then. The common occurrence of washing my laundry in the kitchen sink because I couldn't scrape together a few quarters for the laundromat is a thing of the past. To the shock of all who know me, including myself, I have become a nationally renowned expert in the field of personal finance, specifically retirement planning. My work has been published in more national publications than I can count, and most of this year was spent doing radio and television interviews that reached nationwide audiences and touched millions of people.

I am proud to say that my work has provided me with financial success beyond what my rational mind could have comprehended only a few years prior. The suggestion would have been absurd.

The speed and intensity of my professional (and financial) evolution begs only one question: how exactly did a nobody freelance writer from Anywhere, U.S.A. get here?

This book tells that story. However, the truth is it is not solely mine to tell. This work is a collection of tales that have aided countless people as they prepare for or are already in retirement. This positive impact is where the reward begins and ends for me; the financial success I have experienced from it is nothing more than the cherry on top. The immense wave of change in the world of retirement that has stemmed from my work by placing vital, even lifesaving, information in the hands of those who need it is the true fruit of my labor.

What is this information? Before we delve into the minutia of the material, let's go back two years ago, to the beginning of this journey - when my laundry was regularly washed in the sink and creditors called more often than friends.

Chapter 2
The Call That Changed My Life

Certain events change you. I'm not talking about the trivial events that regularly manifest themselves, like "I lost some weight" or "I have a new boyfriend/girlfriend." These pale in comparison to the life-altering shift that lets us know there is meaning to our existence. This kind of change divides our lives into two parts: everything that happened before it, and everything that's happened since.

This event happened to me on October 6th, more than two years ago. Despite the beautiful sunny but crisp weather that marked this time of year, I hadn't left my apartment all day. I sat at my kitchen table pecking away at my laptop. The current laser-like focus of my attention was an article that was turning out to be the most comprehensive of my professional life thus far. I was working on an in-depth look at the untapped potential of Twitter on the future of finance. Two financial websites were interested in it, and it would earn me a whopping $175 when complete. Considering the contents of my refrigerator were limited to five-day-old Chinese take-out and a vast array of condiments, I was anxious to complete the project and get paid.

After a few hours of intense data mining and writing, I decided it would be a good time for a break. Starbucks was on the next block and the short interlude would allow me to stretch my legs with an excuse to get a cup of Earl Grey.

As I set out on my short walk I grabbed my phone and saw that my mother had left a message. After fumbling with the passcode

I heard the long monologue that was typical of a worried mother calling her 26 year-old daughter. Knowing that my break would not last long, I figured now would be a good time to return her call and get it over with.

My mother answered with her typically jovial "Hello my baby!" We quickly tap danced through the formalities and she attempted to sell me on yet another job opening that would be "perfect for me." I kindly but firmly explained that I loved writing freelance and working on my terms, assuring her that despite the challenges, I was happy.

But my patience had run dry after five minutes of defending my career choice, confirming a lack of future husband prospects, and generating excitement about my brother's new promotion at work.

As I was about to cut her off, she left me with one final thought: "Before you go, I had lunch with Aunt Cindy yesterday and she's not doing well. You should give her a call. She has done so much for you through the years. I think it would be good for you to spend some time with her."

"Is she alright? Is it her health?" I asked.

"No, no. Nothing like that, I just think she could use a friend."

"Of course, I'll call her first chance I get."

We said our goodbyes and hung up. I paused for a moment at my apartment door, worried about my aunt. Finally, I snapped from my trance when I realized how long I had been away from my computer.

Intensely focused on work, my aunt had slipped my mind until the next day. Aunt Cindy was one of my favorite people in the world. At 84 years old, she was actually my great-aunt. My grandmother's sister not only had a biting wit that I found hysterical growing up (anyone that would put my mother in her place in public was alright with me), but it was her depth of compassion and comfort when my father passed away that brought us so close together.

Her trips to visit me at school are among my fondest memories. She would come for the weekend and take me to movies, dinner, and even dancing. There is something surreal about seeing a 90-pound elderly woman dance in a college bar to hip-hop and rap music.

I picked up the phone and called my aunt the next morning.

"Hey Aunt Cindy, it's Sam! How are you?"

"Oh, just fine dear." She gave a long sigh. "Thanks for asking. How about yourself, did you meet Mr. Right yet?"

"You've been talking to my mom, haven't you?"

Aunt Cindy chuckled. "She does have a one track mind, doesn't she?"

"Listen," I changed the subject, "I was thinking about coming for a visit, if you are unarmed, of course." A few years back, she awaited my arrival hiding out of sight with a water gun and proceeded to thoroughly soak not only me, but the bouquet of flowers I had brought as I stepped from the car.

She laughed weakly and agreed to get together. We set up lunch at her home for the next week, made some more small talk, and said our goodbyes.

The day of our lunch my aunt pulled up outside my building in her 2004 Ford Taurus and I climbed into the passenger's seat. She only lived in the next town over, Tinton Falls, but the trip seemed longer than usual; after the usual greetings I felt uncomfortable and broke the extended silence.

"So, how's Joshua?"

She gave a long pause before answering as if awoken from a nap. "He's doing just fine, getting ready for the wedding. He and Jenna booked their honeymoon in Hawaii. I imagine they'll have fun."

Joshua was Aunt Cindy's grandson. Being born within months of each other, Joshua and I spent most of our summers together growing up. His wedding to Jenna, the girl he'd been dating for a little over two years, was scheduled for the spring.

"What about you, dear," Aunt Cindy inquired, "how's your writing career?"

No matter how often I've been asked that question, it never fails to cause me discomfort. Writing is far more to me than a way to earn a living. It isn't a hobby, a job, or even a career. My writing is my art. It's a part of who I am.

"Good," I muttered. "I'm writing a fairly involved exposé on the impact of social media on finance. I have put the better part of six weeks into it and am almost finished. I would love for you to read it."

"That sounds nice dear; I would love to read it when you're finished." Aunt Cindy frowned, deep in thought, and after a few moments asked, "What's social media?" Although her question was a serious one, I couldn't help but burst out laughing.

"You can learn about it when you read my article," I said as I tried to stifle my laughter, "it has to do with computers." "Oh," said Aunt Cindy, cracking the first smile I'd seen, "I never touch the stuff. But if you wrote it, I'm sure I will love it."

After a few more minutes of small talk we arrived at my aunt's sprawling four-acre colonial. Aunt Cindy's house was my home away from home growing up. Joshua and I spent many long summers climbing trees, building forts, digging for treasure, and catching fireflies.

But I walked through the front door to find a living room that was a mere shadow of the place I remembered. My aunt was known for her fastidiousness, but there was no sign of it. The normally well-lit living room was dark, and I detected a hint of mildew.

"Let's get a little light in here." I said.

"Oh," she muttered, "I hadn't noticed."

I went from window to window opening blinds while she ducked into the kitchen to "whip up some lunch." This phrase of hers is a dramatic understatement, as her idea of "whipping up" anything usually consisted of a five-star gourmet meal.

Task complete, I entered the kitchen to find my aunt in her apron chopping asparagus. As soon as she noticed I had entered she handed me a glass of wine and motioned for me to sit. Despite the fact that I could predict her response, I offered to help. As usual, she declined. I parried with my typical insistence and she finally struck the winning blow by jokingly threatening bodily harm using the chef's knife in her hand if I didn't obey her command.

The conversation as she cooked was forced and pointless. We discussed such mundane topics as the weather, a branch that fell from a tree in her enormous back yard, and the neighbor who always complains her Christmas lights are too bright.

Before long, she presented a plate of poached salmon in a lemon dill sauce, steamed asparagus, and rice pilaf. It was a feast by any standard.

Aunt Cindy sat and we bowed our heads to say grace. Upon completion of her prayer, I took delight in digging into the gourmet meal. The quality of the conversation as we ate was in direct contrast to the quality of the repast before us; we said very little, and the tension was welling up inside of me ready to explode like a volcano. Finally, I screwed up the courage to begin.

"So, I spoke with my mother last week."

"Oh yeah?"

"Yup, she told me you weren't doing so well."

My aunt slowly looked up from her plate and stared at me. "What... what did she tell you?"

"Nothing, other than she thought you could use a friend."

"Your mother should learn to mind her own business." she said.

"I think she's just worried about you, Aunt Cindy. I am too. What's wrong?"

"Nothing," she lied.

"I know something's wrong."

"This is none of your concern and I want our visit to be a pleasant one. There is no reason to discuss it! Eat your salmon!"

"But I want to help. What is it?"

"That is very sweet dear, but you can't help. I will take care of it."

"Listen," I pleaded, "When my father died, I always knew I could count on you. You were there for me during the most difficult time of my life. Please, let me return the favor. Maybe I can't help, but if we talk it through together, you might feel better. Whatever it is has got you in knots, I can tell."

She leaned back in her chair with a sigh. Her attempts at remaining stoic were beginning to break.

"Alright, I guess you're gonna find out sooner or later. Probably best it comes from me. I am going to have to sell the house. I just can't afford it anymore."

"What do you mean you have to sell the house?"

"Money has gotten a bit tight around here. The retirement funds your uncle had set up are gone. I have sold just about everything I own over the past few years to survive, and it's not enough. My property taxes and monthly living expenses are unmanageable. Jack and I have discussed it, and my only option is to sell the house and move in with him and…." her face grew tense as she pursed her lips, "her!" It was no secret among the family that my aunt and her daughter-in-law Sheri had never quite seen eye to eye.

"I don't understand. How did this happen? Uncle Frank died

almost five years ago. I thought he had a good pension, life insurance, and you had a lot of money in savings?"

"I really don't know what happened." she sighed. "All I know is that when your uncle retired almost 20 years ago, we were very comfortable. He took care of all the finances and things seemed fine. Once he passed away, it started to get bad. The taxes on this place have gone up dramatically, and don't even get me started on the cost of milk," she said, waving her hand at the small stainless steel creamer on the table. I looked at the exquisite meal spread before me. How could I justify eating salmon when she was complaining about the cost of milk?

Using her remarkable gift to read minds, Aunt Cindy looked at me, "Oh, don't you fret over your meal, my dear. If there is one thing I can afford to do, it's put out a decent meal for my favorite niece when she comes for a visit." I took another bite of my asparagus as to avoid upsetting her, although I no longer enjoyed it.

"What happened to your savings?" I asked.

"Gone," She replied quickly. "The last few years have not served my investments well. What the heck do I know about the stock market?" She sighed. "So, when the market fell and fell and fell recently, I couldn't take it anymore. I was so afraid of losing all my money I sold everything and put my money in guaranteed investments. Well, that was great for a few months when the market went down even more, but these guarantees offered very little interest, at least not enough to live on. So when expenses came due, I would sell some. Eventually, I had to sell them all. This March's property tax bill will be the last of my savings." She paused to take a small bite of her salmon, the first in some time.

"Then, to add insult to injury," she continued, "I saw the market went way up shortly after I sold. It's almost like Wall Street was waiting for your poor old Aunt Cindy to sell everything before it would let people start making money again!" She sounded disgusted.

"The only option I have left is to sell the house your Uncle Frank built over 50 years ago. The house I expected to spend the rest of my days in." She avoided my eyes, made her way over to the kitchen sink, and surveyed the five apple trees in her beautiful, enormous back yard. Uncle Frank had planted a tree to mark the birth of each of their children. Season after season the trees bore fruit that was used for pies, tarts, applesauce, and other delicious homemade delights. Collecting the apples with Joshua as a kid and helping Aunt Cindy bake were some of my fondest memories.

Here was one of the greatest human beings I had ever met. Her existence was an exercise in generosity. At 84, she was afraid of an uncertain future. It didn't make sense. This should not be the last chapter of a remarkable life. I walked up behind my Aunt and gently put my arms around her.

The remainder of my visit was melancholy. We spent much of our time reflecting on the memories that were created in the house. I wondered out loud what kind of family might purchase her home, trying to make her realize how other children would enjoy the vast property for years to come. It only made things worse.

Outside my apartment above Jack's Music Shop, we embraced in a long goodbye and I whispered in her ear, "Don't you worry; I will get you out of this, somehow." She looked at me sternly and said, "No you won't! This is not your problem, Sam. I will be fine. Your Aunt Cindy is a tough old bird. You worry about yourself."

She was right. Finances had always been my Achilles' heel. My lack of financial prowess had been well documented by my creditors. But the burning desire to help remained, regardless of how illogical it seemed.

Chapter 3
My Idea

About a week after my visit to Aunt Cindy's I awoke later than usual, my body sluggish after a long night of tending bar the previous evening. I turned on the television from bed, hoping to find something to jump-start my day. As I flipped quickly through the channels I paused on one with what seemed like an alphabet soup of information running across the bottom of the screen and two "experts" giving wildly opposing opinions on the market and economy. I listened for a few minutes and wondered how anyone without a Master's Degree in finance could comprehend such complicated and apparently ambiguous information. It seemed overwhelming.

Aunt Cindy couldn't be the only retiree facing financial or economic challenges. The state of our economy and the framework of the financial system must have created difficulties for those in a similar position. This would be a story worth telling. It may be too late for my aunt, but perhaps if people can learn from the mistakes she and others like her have made, it would help those planning for their retirement now. My mind was racing as I struggled to develop a strategy for just how I could learn about the mistakes that people made in retirement.

Epiphany! I jumped from my bed and dashed to the bathroom, leaving a trail of clothes I had stripped off along the way. The shower is perhaps the best think tank known to man. I ducked into the steaming hot water and began to formulate a plan.

I spent the next half-hour developing a mental blueprint

of my concept and ironing out wrinkles as the scalding water poured over me. I accepted the fact that in order to thoroughly vet this topic, I would need to speak with retirees from all over the country. I wondered if those in California and Oregon are experiencing different challenges in retirement than those in New Jersey. Regardless, I thought it vital to the integrity of the project that I sample a cross section of the entire country.

I also realized that it was important to meet with these people face-to-face. Finances are not typically an endearing topic to most people. It would be important for me to look these people in the eye if I were to expect them to bare their financial soul.

These two realizations were minor compared to the challenges I still faced. How would I find these people? Would anybody be willing to speak with me? How many is enough? How would I get to their homes? What would I do with all of their stories once I had spoken with them? How could I possibly finance this project?

Despite the seemingly insurmountable obstacles before me, I was determined to push forward.

The next few days were spent on preliminary logistics. The AARP (American Association of Retired Persons) allowed me to run an ad in the next issue of its nationwide magazine asking for volunteers to share their story of financial woe in retirement. Although it would take tremendous coordination to synchronize my eventual appointments to the train schedule, the cost of traveling any other way was just too great. The rails were my only option for this cross-country trek.

The most perplexing question was what to do with my stories once I finished the trip. I attempted to sell the concept to the few publishing houses I had connections with to no avail. There was no interest. Beyond my blog and a few articles, I was unsure of how to best distribute the information once I had collected it. I was confident time would furnish a solution.

Financing the trip was the only remaining hurdle. I used the few weeks' lull that it took for the AARP article to hit homes to scour for cash. I pitched the idea to friends, family, banks, and some wealthy acquaintances. My labors bore little fruit. All told I raised just under $600, a far cry from the $20,000+ required. Not surprisingly, the thought of a 26 year-old needing $20,000 to change the future of retirement must have seemed ludicrous to some people.

Reluctantly, I decided to use the money my father had left me to finance my trip. It was, without a doubt, the hardest decision I had to make regarding the project. I accepted that this money would never be seen again; the project would swallow it whole. I spent the better part of a week wrestling with throwing Dad's last gift to me down a black hole with very little chance of recouping any of it. Ultimately, the memory of my father prevailed; it would have been his choice if he'd still been alive.

The responses from the AARP article started coming in, with a relatively successful 37 individuals and couples across the country who were willing to share their retirement blunders. I was able to set up appointments with 33 of them in 26 states.

The grueling three month course was now set. I purchased an open-ended ticket from Newark's Penn Station to my first stop: a tiny hamlet in upstate New York.

Part II: 10 Tales of Woe

Chapter 4
Elmer Braun

The town of Monroe, NY is small but booming. The exodus of thousands from Manhattan looking for inexpensive real estate was well documented and apparent. This bustling community nestled amongst the towering Catskill Mountains seemed like an appropriate start to the marathon that lay before me.

The trip by taxi from the town's train station to Elmer Braun's home was short and uneventful. Although the town homes first seen by visitors at Garden View Terrace were well kept, as we progressed back through the winding streets they showed signs of disrepair and downright decay. Elmer's address was at the rear of the development.

Not long after I rang the doorbell a short, bald, elderly gentleman answered. He wore a blue button-down shirt that was tucked neatly into his khaki pants with frayed cuffs. He had brown slippers on his feet. His most obvious and distinguishing feature was the tremendous smile on his face.

"Mr. Braun?"

"You must be Sam," he replied, never once losing his addictive grin. "Come in, come in. You must be chilled to the bone. Can I get you a cup of coffee or tea?"

"I would love a cup of tea."

"Of course, that will warm you right up," Elmer replied. He took my coat and hung it on a coat rack.

"So, you're a writer?" Elmer asked as he led me into the kitchen.

"Yes I am."

"Who do you write for?"

"Honestly? Myself mostly. I am freelance at present."

"Freelance, that sounds interesting."

"It really is. I love it. I write what I want, when I want. So, I'm not in a rush to have a boss anytime soon. Although I wish the pay was a little better."

"That sounds wonderful! I'm sure if you keep at it you'll earn a very nice living." He lit the burner and set the teakettle over the flame.

"How about you? What did you do for a living?"

"I was in retail almost my entire life. When I retired I was the manager of the Kmart here in town. I can't say I loved what I did or had any tremendous passion for it the way you obviously do, but it did provide my family with a very comfortable life. I also enjoyed working with people. In fact, that's probably what I miss most about working: the relationships, spending time with my friends and co-workers every day."

I nodded, not really understanding. The life of a freelance writer was a lonely one. I changed the subject.

"How many children do you have, Mr. Braun?" I asked, nodding toward the pictures on the dining room wall that could be seen from the kitchen.

"Oh, you can call me Elmer. Three wonderful kids and ten beautiful grandchildren. I am expecting my first great-grandchild, so I am on cloud nine. They already know it's a boy and have named him, Matthew," he beamed.

"Congratulations!"

"Oh yes, when you reach 86 you will see that each life that enters your family is a gift from God. I intend to enjoy every one of those gifts. But, you didn't come here to talk about my family; you came to talk about my retirement, right?"

"Oh, yes… right. Not that I wouldn't love to talk about your family, you are obviously very blessed."

"Thank you very much. You're a sweetheart. Now, let's sit here at the kitchen table and I can tell you everything you want to know," he suggested.

"Great," I replied. We sat down and I pulled out my digital recorder and writing tablet from my bag.

"So," I began, "as you know, I am going to compile your story with others so people can learn from those mistakes."

"That is a fantastic idea and I am so glad to help."

"Thanks. When we spoke on the phone, you mentioned that you've made some mistakes and retirement has been rocky financially. Tell me, what happened?"

Just then the teapot began to emit a loud whistle. Elmer got up from his chair and scurried across the kitchen, not missing a beat in our conversation, "Don't get me wrong," he began, "I am very happy with my life. Money is really no longer a priority for me. However, I wish I had done some things differently. I know my retirement would be much more comfortable, and I'd be able to spend more time with my family and do more for them. But like most retirees, we had made our share of mistakes that eventually knocked me off track. I am only too grateful that we didn't go through such tough times when Ellen was alive. My wife died at the age of 71 of lung cancer. She was a smoker for years. We both were. I guess it was just her time."

"At any rate, we were set when we first retired. I was 65 and Ellen had never worked, so my retirement became our retirement." He finished adding a little bit of cream to the tea, returned to the table and passed me the steaming mug.

"We had a good nest egg and I had a decent pension. We traveled, spent money on our grandchildren, and we ate out a lot. But we never really lived above our means. That was not an option for the two of us. We have always made that a priority."

"When did you start to have financial trouble?"

He looked into the air, drumming his fingers on the table and said, "Oh, I would say only a few years ago. "Although we planned pretty well, our costs just continued to climb. My pension remained the same, so I was getting squeezed every year. I started dipping more into the investments to make up for the shortfall. They weren't large, but we didn't think we would need them, given my Social Security and pension. We were wrong."

Elmer looked past me and folded his hands. "I honestly think our biggest mistake was when we collected Social Security. We just took it too young."

"I'm not sure I follow," I responded, rapidly jotting notes. "Too early?"

"That's right," Elmer said with a smile as he cupped his hands around his coffee mug. "We wanted our 'free' money from the government so badly, we didn't think about how it would affect our entire financial future. You see, the government gives you the ability to collect Social Security at the age of 62, a little earlier than usual. The benefit is reduced over your lifetime, of course, but hey, I wasn't letting free money sit on the table if I happened to kick the bucket at 64. So, Ellen and I decided to take the reduced benefit from Social Security when we each turned age 62, even though we didn't need the income."

"Why is it a problem to get your money sooner if it's free money?"

"Oh, don't get me wrong, it could have been a very shrewd move. If we both died early in retirement, then absolutely it was the right move. At least then I would have gotten something for the time I was working and paying into Social Security. The point is I didn't look at the big picture. If I died in my 70's, we would have been very well off financially. Sure, we wouldn't have gotten the most out of Uncle Sam, but should that really have been our objective?"

"Sounds like a fair objective to me."

"Perhaps," Elmer said, "or perhaps our objective should have been the most comfortable possible retirement with the least likelihood of running out of money?"

"Alright, I get it. Don't cut off your nose to spite your face."

"Precisely!" Elmer replied. "Sure, the thought of dying early and not taking all that we could from the government seemed too much to bear at the time. But looking back, if we'd died early, who really cares if Social Security won? Did it really improve our lifestyle that much to have an extra $14,000 in income for three additional years?

But, the substantial reduction in our benefit we took by collecting early really has hurt me now. I could do a lot with an extra $600 a month. Social Security income really is the best of all worlds, and Ellen and I cut it short by not focusing on the big picture."

"Wow, I had no idea Social Security income was so complicated. Everyone I have ever talked to has told me to take as much as I can as early as I can."

"Well, my dear," Elmer said, "I am living proof of the danger in that advice." He exhaled hard and sat back in his chair. "I have found a lot of faults in retirement rules of thumb. Every situation is unique. A general rule can get you into trouble at a time when you cannot afford to make mistakes."

"So, what has this mistake cost you?" I asked.

"Simply put, many restful nights' sleep and the ability to do what I want with, and for, my family. But the final price I will pay is yet to be seen. The investments are doing alright now, but if things go south and my portfolio falls, who knows. I may have to move. My independence and even my dignity could be the ultimate price."

The infectious smile that Elmer had worn since I met him was now gone. He stared into his cup. He slowly lifted it to his lips, took a sip, and swallowed hard.

"Elmer, most people who make a mistake, especially financial ones, are embarrassed and don't want to tell anyone. You, however, responded to an ad to tell your mistakes to a complete stranger. Why?"

Elmer looked me in the eye and his smile returned, "Samantha, I'm 86 years old. I've lived a very happy, but fairly modest life. We never could afford to give much money to charities or our church. I did, however, make it a priority that Ellen, the children, and I give of our time and ourselves to worthy causes. What you are doing is a very good thing. People need this information, whether they know it or not. I needed it 20 years ago. If my story can get only one person to think about the consequences of the decisions they make in early retirement, then I will be satisfied. It's important to me that others avoid what I've experienced these last few years, and probably will experience the next few years."

"Well. I thank you for sharing your story. I hope together we can help a lot of people."

Me too, dear," Elmer said gently patting my hand, "Me too!"

The remainder of our visit was spent conversing about his family and love for fly-fishing. Despite his attempts to convince me to stay for just one more cup of tea, Amtrak waits for no one. We concluded our visit with a hug, and on the taxi ride back to the station I became excited about the prospect of meeting more wonderful people like Elmer.

Trip Notes: January 14, 2010

Elmer Braun seemed guilty of only one crime, underestimating his life expectancy. He seemed to have very little fear of living to a ripe old age. Elmer and Ellen were so concerned about getting something, they never thought it could cost him everything.

I am reminded of the Robert Frost poem, "The Road Less Traveled." Often in life we are faced with a road that splits, and we have a decision to make. Unfortunately, the end of either path cannot be seen from our vantage point; however, if we are to proceed forward, we must decide. Sometimes we choose correctly, other times, we do not.

The result of a poor decision may not manifest itself for some time. When faced with a choice, especially in retirement, I have learned today of the importance of removing emotions from that decision. A choice made without logic can very often lead us down the wrong path. It tends to be the impassioned decision that causes us to scratch our head in future years and wonder what we'd been thinking.

Elmer has taught me a very valuable lesson today: In the future, when two roads diverge in the yellow wood, I may not take the one less traveled, but I will certainly keep a level head and think intently about the consequences of my actions before I proceed.

Chapter 5
Jonathan & Florence Abernathe

The clanging of train cars coming to a stop woke me with a start. Shaking off a few moments of confusion, I realized where I was, collected my belongings, and stepped onto the station platform.

So far I'd completed four stops in three days across five states, and the cities were beginning to blur. This was my final stop before a much-needed two-day reprieve. I was exhausted.

Approaching the home of Jonathan and Florence Abernathe of Taylor, MI in the car I'd rented from the train station in Detroit, I noticed the remarkable similarity among the rows of houses. Each was essentially identical to the next, barring a few color changes. It was a glaring reflection of this Mecca of mass production.

I arrived at the address I was given by Mr. Abernathe and was struck by the flawless outdoor decorating, especially impressive given the time of year. I approached the house in the bitter Michigan cold and pressed the doorbell.

The door swung open and I was face to face with a pretty woman whose silver hair was tied in a tight bun behind her head. Her reading glasses were down to the tip of her nose, and she held a Sudoku book and pen. She looked at me a little confused and asked, "May I help you?"

"Are you Florence Abernathe?"

"Yes I am. What can I do for you?"

"My name is Samantha Clason. I spoke with your husband

a few weeks back. He responded to an ad in AARP magazine regarding an article I'm writing about retirement. I am pretty sure we set up an appointment for today?"

"Oh, heavens me," she replied, "was that today? Jon told me about that a few weeks back and it must have slipped both of our minds. Please come in, come in, you must be frozen."

I stepped through the doorway into immediate sensory overload as the aroma of freshly baked cookies coupled with soft music and terrific warmth engulfed me like a blissful tidal wave. As I removed my coat, I noted their elegant living room's overstuffed couches, plush armchair and a crackling fire, far more than just appealing to this weary traveler.

"I'm relieved, you know," Florence whispered as we made our way into the living room. She motioned for me to sit by the fire. "I thought you were a door-to-door saleswoman. I was trying to think of excuses as to why I didn't have time just now," she said with a slight laugh. As I sat, I picked up a magazine to move out of my way and Florence uttered, "I apologize for the mess. We weren't expecting company."

"Oh please, your home is lovely. You should see my apartment," I joked. Her home was immaculate for a day she'd apparently planned to lounge around the house.

"Make yourself comfortable, dear. I am going to get Jonathan and make us some refreshments." She was gone in an instant.

Breathing a deliberate sigh, I sank into the big, cozy, overstuffed cushions of the suede armchair and focused my attention on the crackle of the nearby fire.

Without warning, the door to the kitchen flew open and a short, chubby man in an argyle sweater strutted into the living room. Immediately, I sat up as if I was doing something wrong and Jonathan Abernathe introduced himself.

"I am sorry if there was any confusion about the date, Mr.

Abernathe."

"Don't be silly, it's our fault. In retirement, the days sort of blend together; please, call me Jon."

"You have a lovely home, Jon. How long have you been in Taylor?"

"All my life." He replied as he admired his own living room. "This was my parents' house. We inherited it when they passed away, almost 15 years ago. Their inheritance was the majority of our assets. We got this house and a large amount of General Motors stock. You see, in these parts of Michigan in Dad's day, you put your money in GM stock, not the bank. It was their retirement fund... ours too."

The veil of mystery around the Abernathe's financial blunder was lifted. Despite my lack of knowledge in the field of business, I was well aware that GM had filed for bankruptcy recently. Obviously, this must have hit the couple hard. Unprepared to deal with the topic just yet, I changed the subject.

"So, what did you do for a living, Jon?"

"I worked for GM." he replied. So much for changing the subject. "I was an automotive engineer. I helped during the conceptual design stage, and followed the development through delivery. My design team was responsible for more than 27 different models over my career. I've designed Cadillacs, Hummers, Camaros, and Corvettes. Needless to say, I loved my job. I lived my boyhood dream." He smiled to himself. "My sons loved it too. Bring-your-son-to-work day was especially popular in the Abernathe household."

"I can imagine." I had my recorder out and was writing furiously. Just then, Florence backed through the swinging door with a fully appointed tea and coffee service.

"Tea or coffee for you dear?"

"Tea, thank you." I replied.

"Jonathan is not boring you too much with his car stories, is he? He can go on and on if you let him."

"Oh no," I stammered as I reached for the cup she handed me. "I think it's fascinating."

Jon smiled as he sipped his coffee. "You obviously didn't come to hear war stories about my car designing days. Tell me again, so Flo understands what's going on, what is it you're doing? What is this project all about?"

I delved into the background of the project, my history, and the sad story of an aunt I felt compelled to help. They listened intently until Jon interjected, "Well, I am pretty sure our story will be of some help."

"Tell me."

"I think it's important for you to understand a little about our background." Jon began. "Both of our fathers worked for GM. We lived here, in Taylor, a town where probably 60% of the residents were employed by GM. Growing up, my Dad would take me to the plant where he worked on the assembly line, and I was awestruck by the massive operations. This company was all we knew."

"My parents always taught me the importance of saving. They put money away every month into GM stock. Outside of a few thousand dollars in their checking account, a small bank CD and their home, all of their life's savings was tied up in GM. It was GM stock that made them wealthy in their retirement. Imagine, an uneducated poor kid from Michigan retiring with over $2 million from doing nothing more than working on the assembly line at a car manufacturer. That, my Dad told me, was the power of discipline and investing in GM stock."

"As I mentioned before, my parents passed and I was their only child so I inherited their entire estate. We moved into their house and did nothing with the stock." Jon looked at Flo and gave a short sigh. "Also, as I mentioned I had worked for GM for my entire career and I took my father's advice. I had a sizable amount myself, made up entirely of GM stock." He smiled. "I imagine you can see where I am going with this." I gave an awkward smile in return.

"At its peak, we had almost $4 million in General Motors stock. That would have been more than enough to live on for the rest of our lives, and leave a sizable chunk to the boys. In fact, we even began spending the dividends instead of reinvesting them when we were about five years from retirement, a smart move in hindsight. The dividends alone would have provided us with a very comfortable lifestyle. Then, of course, I imagine you know the rest."

"Could you tell me in your own words?"

"Well, GM fell on hard times the last decade or so. The stock began to fall. They cut the dividend to nothing and eventually went bankrupt. We finally swallowed our pride and sold all of it so we could walk away with something, but our $4 million is now about $120,000. And I guess we were lucky to get even that given that the stock is worthless today."

A swell of nausea overtook me. The thought of a total implosion of two generations of hard work seemed too much to bear. I wasn't exactly sure what to say, but knew I had to say something. "Do you have other assets or income you can live off?"

Florence answered, "Oh sure, there's Social Security, Jon has a pension from work, and I owned a dry cleaning store for almost 20 years that we sold when we decided to retire. Although the majority of our money was in the stock, it wasn't everything."

"However, the $500,000 we are left with to get us through retirement is a lot less than the almost $5 million net worth we had at one point." Jon interjected.

"Oh, stop, Jon. What is the point in crying over spilled milk at this point?"

"I think it's very important for people to understand what happened to us." He defended himself. Jon now turned his attention back to me. "Listen, I honestly don't know if we would have done anything differently. My parents made a lot of money investing in GM. Was their investment a mistake? I really just think we were unlucky."

"Unlucky!" Florence exploded. "Jonathan Abernathe, we lost almost $4 million dollars and you call that unlucky. We obviously did something wrong. Until you understand that fact, it could happen again."

Jon rolled his eyes. It was time I stepped in. "So, whether this was a mistake or just bad luck, what has it cost you?"

Florence immediately began to choke up. Jon noticed and covered for her. "A lot. If we had even half of that money today, our lives would be much different. We could do more with our boys. We could help pay for our grandson's education. We could travel more." Jon was quiet for a moment. "I think the biggest thing we lost is peace of mind. Putting your head on the pillow at night and not worrying about your money is a feeling I took for granted 10 years ago. Once the stock started to hit the skids, it cost me a lot of sleepless nights. Financial peace is something I miss."

Florence interjected, "I agree. Jon and I never lived high on the hog. We never would have spent all that money. Sure, I would have loved to pay for family vacations every year with our children and grandchild or help out with their schooling. But I really miss the level of comfort I'd always felt. That is the true cost for me!"

"Jon, you replied to my ad, correct?" I asked.

"Yes" Jon confirmed.

"Why? I only ask because most people are afraid to talk about their finances, especially their mistakes. You obviously are not."

"First of all, I still think it was just bad luck, not a mistake.

But, I responded because it would have been selfish not to. This terrible thing happened to us in retirement. There is nothing we can do. I can't get my job back, and Flo can't get her business back. It's too late for us to change that. I have always felt that bad things happen for a reason. Maybe our bad experience will help others, and they will do something amazing with their retirement. I would like to be a part of that, even in some small way."

Jon and Florence were gracious hosts. Despite my desire to spend the day with the couple and enjoy some of the creature comforts I'd been deprived of recently, I didn't want to overstay my welcome.

Florence, as if she were sending a grandchild on a long journey, wrapped a paper plate full of cookies and cakes for my trip. I thanked her with a big hug and shook Jon's hand before I headed out into the frigid Michigan winter.

Travel Notes: January 18th 2010

It seems too many people are content to tie their financial future to that of one company or entity. The Abernathe's in Michigan just happened to back the wrong horse. Although Jon did not see fault in this strategy, it seems rather apparent to me that this was nothing more than a gamble.

No doubt, this gamble paid handsome rewards to the generation before him. His father, from very humble beginnings, turned a small salary into a fortune by backing the very same horse that failed his son only a few decades later. Make no mistake; this is what gambling is - an all-or-nothing proposition. High risk; high reward. I, for one, would prefer not to gamble with my retirement. The price paid by the loser can be devastating. It was a price I saw today with my own eyes.

Chapter 6
Julio & Maria Espinoza

The decidedly Mexican décor that flourished throughout the home of Julio and Maria Espinoza was a welcome change from the recent homes I visited. I sat patiently at the kitchen table waiting for Julio to confine their two large German Shepherds to the bedroom. Maria, in a colorful jogging suit that played well off her tanned skin, handed me a glass of water.

"Have you ever been to Oregon, Sam?" Maria asked.

"No. I've never been west of Kentucky, so this trip has been a wonderful experience for me."

"It truly is a beautiful state. If you have some time, take a drive down 101. It hugs the coast and is breathtaking, especially at sunset." She took a long sip of her coffee.

"Sounds great. I may do that."

Julio reappeared at the kitchen door. His clothes were slightly disheveled and soiled, and his previously neatly combed silver hair was ruffled presenting a different impression from the well-groomed man I met when I'd arrived.

"The dogs give you a hard time, dear?" Maria asked.

"Always. But they're fine now." He took a long drink of water. "Are you both ready?"

"Just waiting for you." Maria replied.

Julio sat down. "Where do we begin?"

"Well, like I explained to you on the phone, this project is about vetting retirement mistakes. Why don't we start there?"

"So, our story could help others avoid making the mistakes we made?" Maria questioned.

"That's correct. In my experience, learning from our mistakes is how we learn best. I want to teach those going into retirement about the missteps made by those already well into the process, so they aren't repeated."

"A noble and worthy purpose." Maria commented.

"Well, let's not waste any more time. We'll tell you what happened to us," said Julio. "I was born in Mexico and came over here illegally with my parents at the age of 12. I had very little schooling, but was not afraid to work hard. I started working with my hands at a very young age, picking up odd jobs painting or emptying trash to earn some extra pennies. When I was 16 I found full time work with a construction crew. To say that I was digging ditches most of my young life would be an understatement," he stated with pride.

"I met Maria when I was 18. She was a 17-year-old beauty, born and raised in southern California. We fell in love and got married that year. It was the most important day of my life - I not only won the girl of my dreams, but became a citizen of the greatest country in the world."

Maria picked up the story. "Those early years were difficult. He worked 80-90 hours, seven days a week just to pay the bills. But we were both raised by parents who only knew hard work. For us, it was not an unusual lifestyle."

Julio continued, "We had five children and I continued to work in construction. By my late thirties, I was promoted to foreman. I still worked long hours, but at least I was finally paid well."

"Then in my forties, a co-worker and I started our own construction firm. It was a struggle for the first few years, but the children were mostly grown by then and Maria was able to come work for me, managing the office.

"Over the next 20 years, our business thrived and income was good. We managed to set aside a very nice nest egg along the way. When we finally sold the business and retired in our mid-60's, we had a net worth of about $700,000. Not bad for a Mexican immigrant with no education."

Julio's tone changed. "Look, in my career, I made some mistakes. But whatever I did wrong, I could always overcome it with hard work. Now that Maria and I are in our late 70's, that's not an option. Hard work can't save the day. Unfortunately, our mistakes have been severe."

"What do you mean by that?" I inquired. "It sounds like you were on track for a very comfortable lifestyle."

"We were. The problem, honestly, was my fear." Julio leaned in closer to me. "I worked so hard for my money through the years, I never wanted to risk it. I was so afraid to lose it. In fact, a sizable portion of the money we kept stashed around the house. I wanted to have access to it if there was an emergency. The rest I had in savings accounts and CDs at a couple banks. I always wanted that FDIC insurance, and wouldn't consider anything that wasn't guaranteed. That became a problem."

"I don't understand," I said. "Why exactly was it a problem to insure your money?"

"Well, the problem was that Maria and I had saved a lot of money and worked very hard, but what I realized is that our money wasn't working for us. Sure, we were earning some nice interest back in the '70's and early '80's, but that didn't last long. We were always lenders, never owners. I was so distrusting of the stock market, real estate, and all that stuff that I let it blind me to what I could really accomplish. So, because we knew very little about investing, we played it safe."

"So, what, playing it safe cost you a much better lifestyle?" I asked.

"No, by playing it safe we have risked our current lifestyle.

Our expenses keep growing, but our assets are not. Now, our $700,000 is only about $220,000. We've had to cut back on our wants just to pay for our needs."

"I know you're blaming yourself, but look what happened to all the people that have been in the stock market for the last few years. Many have lost a lot of money. I can't believe you're kicking yourself for playing it safe," I said.

"I've been doing some reading lately, trying to learn about money and investing… I know, better late than never," he joked. "Anyway, it seems to me that those people made the exact opposite mistake. You see, even with the market trouble the last few years, if we had been putting money away since the '60's and had at least some stocks or real estate, we could have had double the nest egg and probably much more. Now, we are paying the price." He shook his head and looked at Maria.

"We try not to overspend," Maria said, "but somehow we've burned through a lot of our savings in only 10 years. The money just seems to be going out so quickly with gas, property taxes… you name it."

"What have you been doing to try to conserve?" I asked.

"Well, for one thing, we stopped traveling. The only traveling we do now is to see our children and grandchildren, who live up and down the coast." Maria replied.

"For me, I love woodworking, but I can't buy the tools I need anymore," Julio added. "I just wish I could go back to work. But the doc says I have a bad back. I think I could do something, but this one," he nudged Maria, "thinks I should listen to my doctor."

I smiled. "I think I would have to agree with Maria. Listen to your doctor. It's just not worth your health. Aside from trips and hobbies, what has this mistake cost you?"

They looked at each other, and Julio sighed. "Our peace of

mind. Being retired is no fun when you are always worried about money. I just wish we had a do-over."

Maria said, "That is the most frustrating part to me. We are so deathly afraid of outliving our money that we scrutinize every expense. I wish I had more time with my children and grandchildren. Our first great-grandchild is due in June. My granddaughter lives in San Diego, and we're worried about how much it's going to cost to go to the christening."

I nodded, then asked my usual last question: "Most people are reluctant to talk about finances with family, let alone a stranger. Why did you respond to the ad?"

Julio answered. "What you are doing is important. I want my kids to know all the mistakes that are possible in retirement. Many of them are already close to retirement and I have talked to them all about my mistakes, but if they can read your article and learn from many others' mistakes, then that would make me feel better. And if someone else can learn from our mistake, then we will have done some good."

We finished up the formal interview and Maria asked me to stay for dinner, but I explained to her that I was on a rigid schedule. I almost changed my mind when she mentioned homemade empanadas, but could not risk missing my next appointment. I left the Espinozas' home, took Maria's advice and drove the scenic Oregon coast via 101.

Travel Notes: February 5th , 2010

The Espinoza's, despite their good intentions and expectations that they were doing all the right things, forgot about one major detail. I remember going to the movies as a kid. The cost was only $4.50. In the 20 years since I now pay $11. What happened?

Obviously our expenses will grow with time, even the young have experienced it to some degree. My astonishment comes from how dramatically it impacted the couple's lifestyle. Inflation is far more than a concern for those who hope for a long retirement, it's a given. There is no avoiding it. We either manage it or wake up one day wondering exactly when it got the better of us.

Chapter 7
Peter & Estelle Graham

The west coast schedule was far more relaxed than my first few weeks. I capitalized on the opportunity to take slow drives along the coast and engage in a little sightseeing. Even though it was winter, the Pacific lost none of its luster.

I arrived in Santa Maria, CA and knocked on the door of apartment 5B of the Fontainebleau Apartments. The smell in the hallway was rank and stale. Timeworn and stained industrial carpet lined the indoor hallways. I doubt the décor had been updated since before I was born. This was not a place I would hope to retire to someday.

Multiple locks on the door clicked and turned and I came face to face with an unkempt elderly woman in a housedress and dirty pink slippers. My first impression of Estelle Graham was not a positive one. But despite her outward appearance, she was pleasant and welcoming as I introduced myself and she led me through the cramped apartment.

"Peter is right over here in the kitchen. Let's go in and we can talk in there."

The apartment smelled of cigar smoke, and there were numerous cats lounging on the furniture. Cheap shades covered the windows and dirty doilies, the tables. I began to worry about the severity of their financial situation. We walked through the tiny living room into an even smaller kitchen.

"Peter!" shouted Estelle, even though he was only a few feet from us. "The writer is here!"

"You don't have to shout!" Peter yelled back. "I'm not deaf." He then turned to me and extended his hand, "Hello, Peter Graham. Welcome to our home!" He said as he vigorously shook my hand.

"Samantha Clason. Call me Sam. Thank you for having me. You have a lovely home," I lied.

"Why thank you," Peter responded with a grin. Estelle gave a loud, "Ha!"

Peter turned to her. "Something you'd like to say, dear?"

"I appreciate your kindness, sweetie. But you should have seen our old house before we moved into this dump. This place is like a Bosnian refugee camp compared to it."

"Really, when did you move?"

"Oh, about a year ago, after Mr. Buffett here lost all our money." Estelle motioned to Peter.

"Wait just a second, I'm not the one who gave all the money to the grandkids to pay for college or got scared and insisted we sell when the market bottomed. That was you, my darling," retorted Peter.

Estelle just rolled her eyes and walked over to the kitchen counter. "Can I get you a cup of coffee or tea, sweetie?"

"Yes, tea would be great, thank you."

"Let's sit down at the table and we can get started. I'm sure you don't want to spend all day listening to us bicker," Peter said.

We sat and I began by offering the usual explanation about my project and how it came to fruition.

"So, now that you can see exactly what I am trying to accomplish, tell me a little about your mistakes. It sounds like you had some trouble in the market?"

"That's an understatement!" replied Peter as he looked over at Estelle.

"What are you looking at me for?" Estelle responded. "It was your fault!"

Peter rolled his eyes, "Here we go again! Yes, I wanted to play the stock market. Yes, I wanted to manage the money. But you were the one that forced me to sell right at the market bottom, and you were the one that gave me heartburn every night the market went down. In all honesty, there is plenty of blame here to go around!"

Estelle turned away from him towards me. "You see dear, I have a very nice pension from the school and we are both drawing Social Security. We thought that should have been enough. We had an additional $500,000 from Peter's 401k that we figured would pay for the niceties. Things like travel, gifts for the grandchildren, that sort of thing," Estelle explained.

Peter interrupted, "We didn't think we needed any help. Most of our income in retirement was guaranteed, and we felt comfortable managing the rest."

"You felt comfortable," Estelle interjected.

"Don't start." Peter grew more aggravated. "The point is, we had all of our money in the stock market in the late '90's. We were retired, but stock prices kept going up and we didn't know any better. Then that tech bubble burst. Our investments took a big hit. After 9/11, we couldn't take the pain and we agreed to sell and put everything in cash. Better to have some than none. So, we sold all of our stocks and our portfolio was worth about $350,000, but no longer losing."

"But sitting in cash never felt right to me. I knew that we were missing out on some great opportunities. I just didn't know what to do. It didn't help that we were so afraid of losing more money. Then in mid-2006, after the market had recovered quite a bit, we got back in. I will take fault for this one. I convinced Estelle that this was our best chance at making some money, and we bought stocks."

"That wound up being a big success for a little while. The market was going up, we did pretty well. Then came the crash.

The market dropped during all that financial mess, and we were worried again. They were talking about the end of the world."

Estelle cut in. "I couldn't take any more losses, and finally told him he had to sell."

"Which was in February 2009," Peter interrupted. "Less than a month before the bottom in the market."

"What can I say; I was afraid of losing all of our money. It just feels like gambling to me. I couldn't take the sleepless nights anymore," Estelle added.

"So there we were, selling into panic twice in 10 years and our $500,000 portfolio was now worth $162,000. We had only used about $60,000 of it the entire time. The rest was lost in the market," Peter concluded.

"Oh, and tell her what we used most of it on," Estelle said, and nudged Peter.

"I was getting there. We gave some money to our granddaughter to pay for her college education. We gave a total of $50,000 to her and were hit with a huge gift tax. We have since learned that we could have paid the money directly to the school to cover the tuition without any tax consequences. We just didn't know the rules. It was very frustrating!"

"Wow, I can imagine." I replied. "How much was the tax?"

"I don't remember exactly, somewhere around $7,000. Just completely wasted money," Peter said.

Estelle added, "Now we're 12 years into our retirement, our expenses seem to keep going up and our income isn't increasing much. Lauren, our granddaughter, came to visit and was selling raffle tickets to raise money for her band uniforms at school. The raffle tickets were $20 a piece and we were out of money that month. I was embarrassed. I had to take a cash advance on my credit card, which cost me another $20, just to get the money to pay for the raffle ticket. We just seem to be running out of money earlier and earlier each month, and neither of us seem to have a clue how to stop it."

"Obviously we had to sell our house," she continued, "which neither of us wanted to do. But we needed the money. Living in this dump should help us survive retirement, but this is not the dream I had imagined."

I figured now was as good a time as any to ask them why they were willing to talk about their financial troubles so openly.

"Sam," Peter answered, "when you get to be our age, you stop caring what other people think. You begin to reflect on what you have done. What will be your legacy? I don't want our legacy to be a string of bad financial decisions. We worked far too hard and have done far too many good things in this life to have that be what people remember. On the other hand, if we can give this difficult time some purpose, some meaning, other than just our daily struggles, then it will be worthwhile. To hell with what others think."

Estelle nodded as Peter spoke. This was the first point the couple agreed on.

"My last question to you is this: What have these mistakes cost you in your retirement?" I asked.

Estelle spoke up. "I'll take this one. It has cost us some material things, which let me tell you dear, do not bring happiness but can add some creature comforts. But it has also affected our relationship and our friendships. We have a circle of friends that go out for dinner every Thursday night to the same restaurant, have for years. It was one of our favorite things to do. About 6 years ago, when money started getting really tight, we had to stop going. We just couldn't afford the $100 bill every week. And although that group is made up of our closest friends, it's not the same. We don't see them often, and I feel like we've fallen outside the clique."

"Beyond that we've lost our freedom, a sense of security,

everything that money can bring," Peter added.

As we wrapped up our conversation, I began to realize that although my first impression of Peter and Estelle was not a favorable one, I developed a soft spot for the couple. Their plight came from a lack of knowledge that not only has affected their lifestyle, but their relationship as well.

We concluded our visit rather shortly after that, and within minutes I was on my way to Los Angeles.

Trip Notes: February 15th, 2010

The day in Santa Maria was enlightening. Peter and Estelle taught me that trying to manage your own investments in retirement is like being a tightrope walker without a net. It matters not if you are perfect 99% of the time; it only takes one slip for things to end badly.

The consequences may be far more than financial. An error in judgment in which one spouse is accountable can have a lasting negative impact on your relationship. Trusting a professional may seem like a big step, but perhaps it is far smaller than the one onto the tightrope.

Chapter 8
Mary Dement

Mary Dement's unique combination of wisdom and spunk had me captivated for 45 minutes during what was usually a five-minute introductory phone call. Although crass at times, she never failed to make me think or laugh. I liked her before I'd even met her.

Rancho Bernardo, a small suburb of San Diego nestled among rolling hills, was Mary's home. I arrived there shortly after 1:30. After my second knock on the front door of her Mexican-style condo, I began to wonder if I was in the wrong place. I rapped on the large oak door once more, this time much louder. Somewhere from within the condo I could hear a voice yelling, "Keep your pants on, I'll be right with you!"

I grew nervous; maybe I had upset her. Another minute passed when I heard some movement from behind the door and it slowly swung open. Before me stood a very thin, white-haired old woman with the biggest smile I had seen since Elmer's back in New York.

"Well hello Sam," she said, as if she had known me for years. "Sorry to make you wait like that, but I was on the toilette and at 84, it's not the routine experience it was when I was your age."

Although I smiled at her candor, I couldn't help but wonder if I really wanted to shake her hand in light of this information. She saved me the embarrassment by putting out her arms and giving me a hug.

"Come on in." She motioned into her beautifully decorated

den. "I'll give you the grand tour before we get to the financial mumbo jumbo. This is my little piece of paradise."

Paradise was no exaggeration; it was a stunning piece of property with a panoramic mountain view from her back patio, which was bordered by individual potted plants and flowers; the garden was peppered with wind chimes, hummingbird feeders, fountains, and a birdbath. It was breathtaking.

"Wow, this is like a little piece of paradise. It's absolutely beautiful."

"What did I tell you?" Mary replied. "When Howard was alive - Howard was my husband - we used to spend so much of our time out here. I would do the gardening and he would read the paper." She sighed. "I miss those days."

"How long ago did he pass?"

"About six years ago. He was 89." She paused. "I can tell by the look on your face that the math seems off. Howard was eleven years older than me. Age doesn't matter if you love someone. Howard was a stallion right up until the very end."

I never heard a woman in her 80's refer to a man as a stallion before. I was speechless.

"Don't laugh dear; someday, you'll be 84 and want a stallion in your life," she said with a grin.

"We really were perfect for each other, though," she continued. "We both loved to travel, we loved fine wines, but most importantly, we both loved martinis. No matter what we were doing, we would stop at 2:00 and have our afternoon martinis. There is nothing like a good stiff drink to get you through your day; it makes life seem less serious somehow. I still have my 2:00 drink every day. In fact, it's almost 2:00 now. Martini time!" She made her way to a tree in the corner of her patio and plucked one of the biggest lemons I've ever seen.

"How do you like your martini, dear?" She shuffle-stepped

back across the patio to the sliding door.

"Oh, none for me thanks." I'd never had a martini before, and was not too keen on drinking while working.

"Oh, don't be silly," she replied. "Are you an alcoholic?"

"No."

"Allergic?"

"No."

"Religious mandate?"

"No," I laughed.

"If you think you are going to get my story without having a drink with me, you're sadly mistaken."

Sitting down for martinis with this incredible woman on a small piece of paradise overlooking the mountains of southern California suddenly seemed like a good idea.

"You win," I said. "However you make it is fine with me."

I followed her into the kitchen where in the corner was a portable bar that was apparently set up strictly for martinis.

Mary took her time. Her martinis were her art. She painstakingly peeled the rind from the fresh lemon, filled a jigger with ice, added gin, splashed in some vermouth, and shook her concoction with both hands. "You know our friends used to call Howard, 'Howtini.' He always made the martinis just right."

She poured her creation into two martini glasses, finished the presentation off with the fresh lemon rind and handed me the drink.

"To living well. Cheers!" she proclaimed, and held up her glass.

"Cheers," I replied.

I helped her tidy up the martini bar and we took our drinks back out to the patio. The two of us spent the next 20 minutes chatting as we absorbed the tranquility.

"Thank you for the drink, Mary. This really is nice."

"Of course, dear. I knew you'd come around," she responded with a sly smile. "I think what you're doing is wonderful. There are too many people like your Aunt Cindy and myself who have royally screwed up and could have used your help years ago. We just didn't know any better. My parents' idea of retirement planning was to take the gold watch, the pension, Social Security, and move in with their kids eventually, making a habit of watching Wheel of Fortune and People's Court. As you can see, I wanted more."

"Tell me, why did you respond to the ad? What's your story?"

"Oh, our story is simple," she began, "Howard and I married late, especially for our generation. I was 32 and he was 43. Since we were both career driven at a young age, we had a nice amount saved when we combined our funds. We really expected that retirement would not be a problem. Howard worked at the naval base, and the pension we received from his job was a comfortable one. Our problem came from our overspending. We had a financial guy who told us many times that we were spending too much. We just didn't care. We were enjoying our life.

"We took extravagant trips," she continued, "drank fine wines, bought our kids and grandchildren nice presents for birthdays and holidays. We spared no expense." Her smile began to fade. "We just never lived for the future. Our motto was, "We could be dead tomorrow and we are enjoying what we've earned."

"For Howard, that was fine. He was older and passed away before the money really became a problem. What we ignored was not how we might regret spending the money if we became sick or disabled; it was, what if we had good health right into our 90's? We just didn't consider the risk of living too long."

She put her martini down on the end table. After walking very slow and deliberately across the patio, Mary picked up a small bag of birdseed and began filling the small plastic tube of the birdfeeder.

"So, here I am, 84 years old and almost out of money. I am not sure if I will be able to continue to afford the condo any longer. I haven't spoken to my daughter about this, but I know what her answer will be, to move in with her." Reaching into her bag of seed, she grabbed a small handful and spread it on the grass just off the side of the patio. Instantly, countless birds flocked to the area and took advantage of the free buffet.

"Don't get me wrong, I love my daughter and the kids, but she lives in North Dakota. She divorced her husband about five years ago, and I cannot stand the man she currently lives with. He's a real jerk. I've told my daughter many times she is a fool for living with a man with her kids in the house, but she doesn't listen." She wrapped up the remaining birdseed, returned it to the spot she originally got it, and reclaimed her seat next to me.

"So, that's it in a nutshell, dear. Howard and I really blew it. I don't regret our life and the fun we had; I only wish we were more creative at containing the expenses. Looking back, the joy we took came from being together, experiencing things together. We could have found the same joy drinking $15 bottles of wine instead of $150 bottles. I know we could have taken the same trips all over the world at a cheaper price if we only would have been a little more cost conscious." She sighed. "That was just never our mentality. We never thought about where we would be down the road. We knew what we had to do, we just didn't do it. That is what causes me to lose sleep at night, the regret."

I listened and nodded as she spoke. When I realized she was finished with her story, I asked, "What do you think the mistakes you made with your money have cost you?"

Looking at me, she took a deep breath, and said, "Oh, I don't know. Like I said, I don't regret the time I spent with Howard and all the wonderful things we did together. I do regret the way we did them. If we were a little more careful with our money, today I could be enjoying my life worry-free. You never stop worrying, dear. I worry about my children, grandchildren, friends, whether my back is going to hurt like hell in the morning, but the worry I have felt recently about money and my uncertain future has been especially difficult. I am tired of being afraid all the time. I'm afraid of my future. That is a scary place when you're 84. I don't want to lose my independence."

She took her last sip of martini. "Another martini, dear?"

Oh God no, I thought to myself. I was already feeling a pretty strong buzz from the four sips I'd had, and was staring at half a glass remaining. "No thank you," I replied. "I have to drive."

"You have to drive? Where are you going so soon?" she inquired.

"I have to get back to my hotel eventually. I have another appointment tomorrow afternoon in San Marcos."

"My dear Samantha, you are 27 years old and have been on the road now for over six weeks, sleeping on trains and in flea bag motels. San Marcos is less than 30 minutes from here. You are going to stay with me tonight. You can have the spare bedroom, and I am going to make you a home cooked meal."

"Oh, Mary, thank you very much, but I couldn't," I lied. I was exhausted, and tired of life on the road. The motel beds were uncomfortable, fast food was getting boring, and a lack of companionship made me lonely. The thought of spending more time with Mary sounded just about perfect. But, I couldn't impose.

"Don't even think about it. You call your hotel right now and cancel your room. Save yourself the money and then we can have another drink before we go to the grocery store. I just need a few things for dinner."

I had to accept the fact that Mary might have just wanted a martini buddy for the night. However, I was not above being used for my liver. "Alright, I'll agree on one condition - you let me buy the groceries for dinner."

"Don't be silly. You are my guest. I'll take care of dinner."

"Nope, that's my only condition. You are saving me almost $80 on the hotel room, so the least I can do is pay for dinner."

She gave me a rather stern look, then smiled. "You're a tough negotiator for someone so young. It's a deal."

So, the matter was settled and I was overjoyed. I conceded to one more martini, knowing full well the hydrangeas on my right would be the beneficiary of the refilled glass. I only hoped martinis didn't kill plants.

We spent another hour talking, laughing, and just enjoying being together. She was, without a doubt, the closest thing to a friend I had found on my trip.

We spent the rest of the afternoon grocery shopping. She planned an elaborate dinner of roasted duck in a red wine and rosemary sauce, garlic mashed potatoes, and asparagus with hollandaise. Mary also picked up two bottles of a delicious Pinot Noir (which she insisted on paying for). The way she put it, one was for the duck and one was for us. She spared none of her finest china and linens. The table looked like it had been set for an elaborate wedding. "I'm 84 years old; every occasion is special." Perhaps it was the four drinks I now had ingested, but Mary made a lot of sense.

Everything about the feast was perfect: the wine, food, and conversation. For the first time in a while, I was comfortable and happy.

We indulged in our dessert of gourmet chocolates and port wine on the patio overlooking the twinkling lights in the distant mountains. We talked more, and finally decided to turn in just after midnight.

I enjoyed being doted on, and it was obvious she enjoyed having someone to dote on. Leaving tomorrow would not be easy. I was going to miss Mary!

Trip Notes: February 21st, 2010

What an incredible visit with an incredible woman. The time I spent in San Diego was much needed. The companionship and the weather helped recharge my batteries.

Mary was caught in a financial mistake that is all too common in our society. Mary and her husband were guilty of living on credit. I don't mean credit in the traditional sense, the type of debt I have found myself in over the past few years. Instead of borrowing from a credit card or bank, Mary & Howard borrowed from her future. The couple spent the early years of their retirement living far beyond their means. Often, they would cling to the maxim of "we could be gone tomorrow, so live every day like it's you're last." Those who live by this creed often find the real risk is not in dying too soon, but living too long.

It seems more likely that to experience all that is available to us and appreciate what is before us each day is the genuine intention of the quote. It is difficult to fathom that whoever originally suggested it meant we should mortgage our future by splurging today.

Chapter 9
Marion Ritchie

The front door swung open and in front of me stood a stout woman wearing a bathrobe and slippers. She wore no make-up and the lines on her face were deep and pronounced, marking her many years. Despite my call to confirm yesterday, she looked at me as if she had no idea who I was.

"May I help you?" she asked through the storm door.

"Are you Marion Ritchie?"

"Yes. What can I do for you?"

"Hi Marion. I'm Samantha Clason, the writer. We spoke on the phone yesterday."

"We did?" She brought her hand to her forehead. "I'm sorry, please come in."

She offered to take my coat and motioned to enter the living room. Marion's home, located in Henderson, Nevada, was obviously beautiful at one time but was now decaying. The plaster walls were cracked, and the paint was dull. Her furniture was worn and a few pieces sported mismatched slipcovers. Collectible plates of famous cartoon characters on display throughout the home completed the décor.

"I am sorry if I forgot our appointment. My mind is not as good as it used to be. Please, take a seat." She motioned to the sofa. "Can I get you anything, Sam? Coffee, soft drink, water?"

"No thank you, I'm fine." I grew concerned about her memory as I took out my note pad. Perhaps she was in the early stages of dementia or Alzheimer's, in which case it would be a waste of time to discuss topics that occurred years ago if she couldn't remember our phone conversation from yesterday.

"So, I remember speaking with you on the phone a few weeks ago, but tell me a little about this project of yours." She asked.

As I had so many times before, I told her in detail about my background, Aunt Cindy, and the trip. She nodded her head and listened intently.

After I filled in the back-story, I thought it was important to be honest. "Marion, I take it you see the importance of what I am doing here. I know you have a story to share, but will you be able to remember it? I am sorry for being so candid, but I'm concerned."

"I know, I'm sorry about that. Things have been slipping my mind a lot lately. It's been getting worse over the past six months or so. However, one thing I can assure you is that it is only a problem with short-term memory. I can remember what happened last year or when I was a child as clear as day, but ask me where I ate lunch yesterday and I may not be able to tell you. Don't get old, Sam. It's no fun!"

I grinned. "Alright, so you remember why you responded to the ad in AARP magazine?"

"Of course, I could never forget that story."

"Great, so let's get to it. Tell me about what happened to you, the mistake you made with your finances in retirement."

"Well, let me start by telling you that Jack, my husband, died about four years ago. He was a wonderful man and I miss him every day, but he was the one who handled the finances. He took care of the bank accounts, savings, investments, everything. In fact, the biggest mistake we made was not getting me more involved in the daily finances of the household. When Jack died, I didn't even know which banks our money was with or what investments we had. It was very sloppy planning, and we were both to blame.

"After Jack died, my son spent three weeks with me helping with the funeral arrangements, but more importantly, helping track down the money. It took some time, but we found all the accounts and the assets. Every time one problem was solved, a new one came up. I realized right away I was in over my head and needed help."

"I decided that I would start looking for a professional. Jack had always resisted hiring someone to help us with our money. He thought they were all crooks, but I really just think he was stubborn. It was hard enough to get him to stop and ask for directions when we were lost or call a plumber when the pipes were leaking; men just do not know how to ask for help." She smiled and winked.

"Conveniently enough," she continued, "about a month after Jack died I received an invitation for a free dinner and financial education held by a very prominent financial firm. Since I was in the market for some financial help anyway, I figured I should attend and see what they had to say. So, I went to their dinner at a lovely restaurant. I was in the room with about 25 other retirees who were all out to learn how to live off their money. We had a wonderful dinner, and the presenter was this very handsome gentleman in his 40's who was an eloquent speaker. He told us all about how the stock market was one big casino and how his industry had figured out a way to provide us with the upside of the market with little or no downside risk. The product was a variable annuity. Well, let me tell you, I was hooked."

"He said everything I wanted to hear and made it all sound so perfect. I made an appointment to see him at his office and we discussed how much money I had to invest, which was about a million dollars at the time. We also talked about the house. He mentioned that there would be tax benefits if I refinanced, took that money and put it into the annuity. I listened and did everything he told me. I took a new mortgage on the house for about $250,000 and then sold all of my investments and used every dime to buy this annuity. I had about $1.25 million tied up with this guy, and only about $20,000 in cash on hand.

"For the first time since Jack died, I felt comfortable financially. I finally felt that I could rest. My money was in good hands. Boy, was I wrong!"

"Wrong? What do you mean, what happened?" I asked.

"It started when I received my first statement. I was under the impression that the account could never lose money. However, when I received my first statement, I was shocked. The account had lost almost $25,000. I didn't know why, it was very unclear. I called the gentleman who had sold me the annuity and he was unavailable. So I left him a message. He still hadn't called me back, so I left him another message. Finally, three days after my original phone call, he returned my call and told me the reduction in value was for fees and expenses, but as long as I kept the annuity intact for 10 years, that reduction would not be permanent."

"10 years?" I responded. "Seriously?"

"I know, I thought the same thing. I told him, I can't keep the money in there for 10 years. I need it to live. He told me not to worry, it was still a great tax shelter and that it would provide me with what I was looking for," she said as she rolled her eyes.

"So, the next month," she continued, "I wanted to give some money to my daughter. Her husband got laid off and they asked for a small loan to help get her through a tough period. I called my advisor and couldn't get him. By this time, I wasn't surprised, but the kids needed the money soon, so I left a heated message and he called me the next day. I told him that I needed about $40,000 and he said that he would recommend against pulling out that much money so soon. The penalties would be large.

"Now, I was upset," she said. "I trusted this man with my money, thinking he would do what was right for me and be attentive to my needs. He was none of those things. I even questioned if he knew anything about money or retirement other than how to sell annuities."

"Sounds like you got ripped off," I said.

"No, not so much ripped off, but more like taken advantage of. He did not scam me. I signed the papers, I made the decision, I should have known better. He took advantage of my lack of knowledge. I truly think that he believed he was doing what was best for me. The problem was, he never asked about me, my goals, my beliefs about money, my background. All he cared about was putting me in that annuity."

"So what did you do?" I asked.

"I had just about had it with this 'advisor.' I talked to a few of my friends and asked them if they had any good recommendations. My friend Alice told me about her financial planner, who did not sell anything. He was a 'fee-only' planner."

"What does that mean?"

"A fee-only planner is an advisor who doesn't earn a commission from selling financial products. You pay them for their advice, nothing more."

"Got it." I jotted down a few notes.

"That sounded like what I was looking for, so I met with this gentleman, and hired him to help me."

"Just like that?"

"Well, the courting process was not that simple, but I figured I would be brief in the interest of time and your wrist," she chuckled and motioned to my scribbling notes on my notepad.

"Rick, my new CFP®, told me that the variable annuity was a bad move for someone in my position, and refinancing the house was definitely something I should not have done."

I'm sorry CFP®? I interrupted.

"A CFP® means Certified Financial Planner. Apparently, that is what I should have been looking for all along. It just means that they have some higher level of education and experience in these things."

"I've never heard of it before," I responded.

"Me neither. I wish I knew about it before I hired the guy who sold me the annuity."

"So, what happened next?" I asked.

"Well, what could I do? Rick told me that just because I made a bad decision in the past doesn't mean that I should stick with it and ride it out. The fees were hefty, but I needed to cut my losses and move forward. So, that's what I did. I cashed in the annuity, took a 10% hit to the tune of $125,000. Rick had me pay back the mortgage, and he invested the rest in a diversified portfolio that leaves a fair amount in cash to manage my monthly expenses."

"All in all, that mistake cost me almost $135,000 if you consider the fees to take out the mortgage. It was an expensive but valuable lesson. Believe me, I am not happy to have lost $135,000, but at least it didn't bankrupt me. I look at those poor people who lost their entire life savings to Bernie Madoff, and I count my blessings that my mistake was only 10% of my assets. You have to look at the bright side, right?"

"Do you have any recourse with the annuity salesman… legally, I mean?" I asked.

"No, he did nothing illegal. Immoral perhaps, but not illegal." she said, a little embarrassed. "I chalk it up to a very expensive lesson learned. Rick is wonderful; he is always available to help me. He gives me honest, objective advice, and I am never worried he has ulterior motives."

"Well, sounds like it all worked out, then?"

"For the most part, yes, I am blessed."

"Marion, what do you think this mistake has cost you in your life?"

"I know exactly, it cost me $135,000!" she replied with a smile.

I laughed. "I guess that's true."

"Seriously, I really don't see the loss as costing me anything. More like paid education. I learned a lot from that mistake. It is a mistake I wish I'd made when I was much younger and with less money, but I am not going to beat myself up over it. My philosophy is, bad things and mistakes happen in our lives. We can either let regret eat us alive, or we can learn from those mistakes and move on. That is what I have chosen to do."

"Great philosophy! It's so true."

Marion and I spent the remainder of our time together discussing the stock market and the economy. These were two topics I never thought I would be discussing with a 71-year-old, but Marion had invested a lot of time in educating herself about these topics since her experience with the annuity salesman. She was obviously excited to show off her new knowledge.

Trip Notes: March 2nd, 2010

I completed my tour of the west coast by spending the afternoon with a sweet lady in Henderson, NV. Marion, it seems to me, was guilty of nothing more than being naïve. I think we've all been accused of this at some point. Often, as we try to accomplish something we have never attempted before, we fail due to a lack of knowledge. It can be our own fault, but frequently it is someone else who takes advantage of our inexperience.

My Aunt Cindy's story made me aware of the complexities of managing one's finances, but Marion has now made me aware of the complexities of the varying degree of professionals. I had no idea that all financial professionals were not created equal.

Chapter 10
Reese & Emma Manning

After many weeks in a rental car, I was riding the rails again. Although I relished the freedom of driving, it was equally satisfying to have extra time to work. The train would also allow for more down time as I headed back east. Next stop: Texas!

Reese and Emma Manning lived in downtown Dallas, their home was an apartment above a massive retail center the two entrepreneurs had opened decades before. Emma graciously welcomed me inside.

"Did you have any trouble finding the place, Sam?" She asked as she closed the door behind me.

"No, not really. I must say I was a little startled when I saw the address was a storefront. I thought I was in the wrong place."

"Oh, I'm sorry. I should have mentioned that to you. Reese and I opened that store just over 50 years ago. We bought the building, and have lived above it ever since. Our sons run it now. At first it was to save money while the store got off the ground. Then it just became convenient. Short commute, ya know."

We walked through the spacious living room and I was immediately drawn to the oversized windows with a view of downtown Dallas.

Emma walked up next to me and pointed. "Do you see that building there?"

"Yup," I replied.

"That's the Texas Book Depository that Lee Harvey Oswald shot Kennedy from."

"Wow. Is it really?"

"That's right. Three blocks away, to be exact. Reese and I had only opened the store a few years prior and were working that day. It was absolute mayhem. Police were everywhere during the manhunt. They even searched our store."

"Unbelievable. That must have been a scary time."

"It was. It was so sad and frightening." We stared out the windows a few moments longer. "I figured we could talk in the kitchen," she said in her heavy Texas drawl. "Reese is in there now finishing up some paperwork."

We walked under an archway to where a chubby bald man with reading glasses sat at the kitchen table, writing among papers that were strewn about. As soon as he saw us, he jumped from his seat and walked over to me with his hand extended. "Reese Manning! You must be the reporter, Samantha?"

"Please, call me Sam. I'm not a reporter. Just a freelance writer."

"I apologize. I hope I didn't offend you." He stated with his strong Texas accent.

"Oh no, not at all. I would love to be a reporter! Reporters get a paycheck. I don't. You have a beautiful home, Mr. Manning."

"Please, call me Reese. And thank you. The credit goes to Emma. She does such a great job of taking care of the place. My job is to call the plumber if there is a leaky pipe or an electrician for a faulty socket. The good Lord blessed me with the business gene, not the handyman gene."

"As long as we are blessed with something, who are we to complain, right?" I said.

"You are absolutely right, darlin'."

"So," Emma interjected, "you're here to learn about our retirement mistakes, right?"

"That's right. I am speaking with more than 30 retirees."

"Well, we have a whopper for you," Reese said.

"Don't say that, Reese," Emma cut him off. "It's not a whopper, just a mistake. I think other people are far worse off than us."

"No doubt," agreed Reese, "but that doesn't mean it wasn't a whopper to us."

"So tell me," I interjected, "what was the mistake?"

"Well," Reese began, "we've owned this store below us for over 50 years. It took about 10 years before we were earning any kind of profit. Ironically, profits didn't really come until the early '70's, when the economy wasn't great. But, once we started making money, things stayed pretty good. So, we wanted to be smart and invest it. Our opinion was to just put the money away and let it grow. That's what we were always told. I had a good friend who was in the investment industry, and we called him to handle it."

"Phil, that's our friend, started investing in stocks in the '70's and then moved us to mutual funds in the '80's. He seemed to know what he was doing, but our investments never seemed to make much money. I wasn't paying attention to it through most of the '70's when I was focused on the store, but when the market started doing very well in the '80's and retirement was just around the corner, I became more involved."

"I take it things didn't go so well in the '80's?" I asked.

"Well, the account did alright, I guess," Reese responded. "But it never seemed to do as well as the market. We were invested all in stocks during that period. The market went up 18% and we'd get 14%, or it would go up 6% and we'd get 3%. No matter what the market did, we were underperforming consistently."

"The amazing thing is, I never would have even realized it if it weren't for this three-day investment seminar I took in 1986. The instructor asked all the people in the class to bring in their statements. He taught us how to read a statement and know exactly what we were paying in our expenses."

"What do you mean by expenses?" I asked.

"Those are the costs to invest. It's not free, which some people think. But the investing world is sneaky. They bury your fees so you don't see them. The costs used to be mainly on securities traded, which means I would pay a commission if I bought 100 shares of IBM. Those costs, although they're still around, are dirt-cheap today. In fact, the average American doesn't own individual shares anyway. They invest in mutual funds. That's what we've mostly invested in since the '80's."

"But the wrong mutual fund can be very expensive. So, I learned that day that we had been paying over 3% per year in fees and expenses to everyone from our financial advisor to the mutual funds we were invested in. We were even paying almost half a percent to the mutual fund's marketing costs! Can you believe that?"

"Well, 3% doesn't sound too bad. Is that high?"

"Oh yes," chimed in Emma. "Think about it like this: Assume you have $100,000 invested and you are trying to earn $8,000 per year. The finance industry is going to take $3,000 of that $8,000. Do you think that's fair? How about if it was a million dollars and they were going to take $30,000 of your $80,000?"

"Wow, I never thought of it like that," I said. "So, what did you do?"

"I started to learn," Reese replied. "I began to read everything I could get my hands on that discussed investments. I watched CNBC and read The Wall Street Journal daily. I learned very quickly that the 3% I was paying was not only adding no value to my return, but it was actually hurting my investment performance. I'll bet you will never guess over the years how much it was hurting it by?"

"I have no clue," I said.

"Those costs created an underperformance of a little more than 3%," Reese quickly answered.

"Really? That seems like a coincidence."

"It's no coincidence," he corrected me. "Statistics have shown that the cost you pay to manage your money is roughly how much you will underperform in the market, on average. Although there was nothing illegal going on, we were getting ripped off. We calculated that the 3%, compounded every year that we were paying Phil for over 25 years, cost us over $200,000." He paused for dramatic emphasis. "Could you imagine? We did not even know what this gradual siphoning of money every year was costing us in retirement. We didn't even know it was happening."

"So, what did you do to fix it?" I asked.

"Well, first we fired our so-called 'friend.'" Reese had daggers in his eyes. "Anyone doing that to us was no friend of mine. Then, we found the right kind of financial planner that we could work with who charged appropriately and kept a close eye on our expenses. We now pay about 1.5% for everything. That includes services we didn't have before like financial planning, taxes, and a whole lot more. We are working with someone whose interests are better aligned with our own. That helps us sleep better at night."

"I like him a lot better, too," Emma interjected. "I don't get that feeling like he's trying to sell us anything. I know I can trust his advice. He's also easy to talk to and returns our phone calls. I know, that sounds silly, but it really is a refreshing change."

"What do you think this mistake has cost you?"

"$223,456… according to my new financial planner," Reese answered without hesitation. "And I'm pissed about every dime."

"We're fine," Emma said. "We still get a nice income from the store and have a decent savings. We'll never want for anything. The money is secondary to me. It's the fact that these fees were never disclosed unless you read the 82-page prospectus. We had no idea what we were paying, or that we should even look out for this. We both just feel taken… and by a friend, no less."

As I wrapped up and prepared to leave, Emma asked if I would like to take a walk over to the area where Kennedy was shot and tour the Texas Book Depository, which was now a museum. I jumped at the chance to have a guided tour of this historic landmark by a woman who was there that terrible day.

I repaid Emma's kindness by taking her to dinner. I had never experienced authentic Tex-Mex, and was delighted by the prospect. Just before leaving, Emma hugged me and wished me well. I promised to keep in touch, exchanging email addresses, and within minutes I was in a cab headed back to the Dallas train station.

Trip Notes: March 13th, 2010

Reese & Emma were not plagued by the regret that most of those I have visited had experienced. Although their retirement error had cost them a large sum of money, it didn't destroy their retirement. What I learned from their tale was the importance of the details. It's the little aspects in everything we do that can have a great impact.

Just as a bricklayer can build a house one small block at a time, so too can an investment account grow. However, if each time a bricklayer lays five bricks, two are removed, the construction would progress at a sluggish rate. Know what you pay in fees and expenses. Knowledge is power.

Chapter 11
Bill Lancaster

Bill Lancaster, a 75-year-old bachelor in Deerfield Beach, FL wore a stained white V-neck tee and spoke very little as he led me through his small, cluttered condo to the kitchen. "Is this alright?" he asked as he attempted to clear away some newspapers, plates, and an old coffee cup from a folding table.

"It's fine, thanks." I sat down.

Bill is a lifetime bachelor with no children. He lived in Brooklyn, NY most of his life but moved to Florida when he retired from the police force at the age of 62.

"Retirement mistakes, huh? You've come to the right house. I've made 'em all." He said through a heavy Brooklyn accent. "I am darn near broke now because of my mistakes. The only money I survive on now is my police pension and Social Security. Thank God for both of those. I lost everything else in the market."

"Really?" I asked. "You lost all of your money in the market?"

"Oh sure. The market is just one big casino in my opinion. I used to watch CNBC, listen to all those "know-it-alls" tell me their opinion and I would do what they said. There were many times I got a hot tip from a friend who knew someone in the business. Either way, I'd get screwed. Oh, I won a few big ones in my day, but more often I lost."

"The worst part was my timing. As soon as I'd buy the stock, it would go down. Once I sold it, it would go up. That happened to me, like, a hundred times. I was really bad at timing that stuff."

"How much money did you lose?"

"Oh, I don't know, maybe $300,000. Boy, when you say it like that it sounds like a lot of money, huh?"

"I'm not quite sure how you could say it where it wouldn't sound like a lot of money."

"True! I don't know, I'm kinda used to the big wins and losses. I've always been a bit of a gambler. I love casinos, the track, poker rooms. I even gamble a little online now. I have cut back quite a bit because money has been so tight lately. Oh well, easy come, easy go, right?"

"I guess. Did it really come that easy?"

"Well, I inherited about $60,000 from my mother. The rest I saved during my working years. I guess it wasn't so easy."

"Tell me, how has this mistake affected your retirement?" I asked.

"Well, I would be $300,000 richer," he said without cracking a smile. "I guess I can't do the things I want to do. I love fishing. All through my years on the force, I would spend my weekends in the summer fishing right off the beach. I took at least one deep sea fishing trip each year. Since money's been so tight, I haven't been able to fish, not even off the coast."

"I'm sorry, maybe I'm not understanding something. The cost to fish off the coast must be almost nothing, right?"

"Oh, my pole broke a few years back and I haven't had the money for a new one. If I can't afford a new pole, I certainly can't afford deep sea fishing trips on a chartered boat.

"I also would do more traveling," he continued. "I used to love to go to Vegas and skiing in Colorado. I'm too old to ski, but I wish I could go out and visit those places again, nonetheless. I really miss traveling."

"Bill, most people don't talk about money, especially to strangers and especially about their mistakes. You, however, chose to pick up the phone and make an appointment to talk with me; share your financial mistake. Why?"

"Oh, I don't know. I guess it's just nice to have someone to talk to. I've never been afraid to talk about money. On the force, we always talked about money problems; I didn't feel weird or nothin', you know. I just figured I had something to share that might help someone else." He shrugged.

"Well, I'm glad you did. I'm sure this will be very helpful to a lot of people."

"You think? Do you think my mess might actually help someone?" he responded, and his face lit up.

"I really do."

Trip Notes: March 25th, 2010

I met a sad old man today named Bill. I got the impression that he always looked for a short cut, the easy way out. I could picture him sitting at a card table looking for his next big score. What he fails to recognize is that the only consistent winner is the casino. They have the advantage against the player. Bill plays a loser's game, but doesn't seem to understand why he lost. This mentality is common. Consistency is boring; big wins get all the attention.

Chapter 12
Tom & Judith Kelly

Life has been a struggle lately for Judith Kelly. As if poor knees and waning vision weren't enough, Judith's husband Tom was admitted into a nursing facility almost eight years ago after a diagnosis of Alzheimer's disease. She now spends most of her time at her modest home in Garden City, a small suburb of Savannah, GA, sitting on her front porch, sipping sweet tea, and reading tabloid magazines.

"Well, we retired about 11 years ago now, when we were both 65," she began. "Tom had a small pension and we had substantial savings to the tune of almost $400,000. We only really had about a year of really nice carefree retirement. Then, Tom started forgetting things. It was gradual at first, car keys, passwords, bank account numbers. But he just kept getting worse. He was forgetting our children and grandchildren's names. This was not a slip or a split second trouble recalling; he didn't know who they were. Finally, one night I walked into the bedroom and he asked who I was. I knew he couldn't put off seeing a doctor any longer.

"It took about another year for him to deteriorate so badly that I just couldn't take care of him anymore. I had no choice but to check him into a long-term care facility. He's been there now for almost six years. It's hard."

"How bad is the Alzheimer's at this point?" I asked.

"Bad," she replied. "He doesn't recognize any of his family anymore. His favorite thing to do is play with his G.I. Joes." She fought back tears. "I used to visit him every day, but I just can't anymore. I now see him only twice a week. I can't help but think that I'm a bad person, but the man I love, the man I have spent 52 years of my life with, the man who is the father of my children, the man who is my soul mate, doesn't even recognize me. He doesn't remember that I was even there a mere few days before. When I go, I don't even think I am providing him with any comfort." She said as tears streamed down her face.

I reached out for her hand. "You can't feel guilty. You've been put in an impossible position. He is getting the care he needs, and you need to take care of yourself."

"Thank you. I know you're right, but I can't help but feel like I've let him down." She reached for a tissue.

"Think about it if things were reversed and you were in the facility. You didn't remember anything that had happened in the last 60 years. Would you want Tom spending his golden years visiting you and dealing with all that pain?"

"Of course not," she replied.

"Then do you think Tom wants this for you? Of course he doesn't. You are a good person in a very difficult situation."

"Well, thank you dear, I really appreciate the kind words," she said, looking down at my hand as she patted it.

"You're not here to hear my sob story about Tom's illness. You're here to hear my sob story about our finances," she said with a chuckle. "Unfortunately, even though we shopped around, the facility where Tom is staying is not cheap, and the price goes up every year. The costs have really dwindled our savings. At this rate, I only have about a year's worth of expenses left in savings. I don't know what I am going to do."

"What about the government? Is there any aid you are eligible for?" I asked.

"There will be. I did my research years back and try to stay on top of the Medicaid laws, but unfortunately we're not eligible until a little more money is gone. What I am worried most about is that Tom will need to move facilities. The one he's in now doesn't take Medicaid. I'm very happy with his current home; the people there all know me and even give me special privileges at times. They treat Tom well. I don't know what will happen if we move him to a Medicaid approved facility."

"I've decided to keep Tom there as long as I can afford to. I don't even want to apply for Medicaid until there is no choice. Which means next year I will need to put the house up for sale. I just won't be able to afford this place anymore. We've lived here 50 years." She picked up her teacup, stood up, and walked towards the sink. It was obvious she didn't want me to see her cry.

"What are you going to do?" I asked.

"Oh, I'll be fine. I'll rent a one-bedroom place. I'll be able to afford that on my Social Security." She sighed, looked around the kitchen. "Probably for the best, to be honest with you. I can't much keep up this 'ole place anyway. I need something smaller with less work."

Her argument was not convincing anyone, not even herself.

"Judith, I'm curious. The ad I ran in AARP asked for retirement mistakes. How is this a mistake? I mean, what really could you have done to prevent this?"

She looked up at me, "Well, the one mistake we made, which obviously turned out to be a big one, was that we didn't get any long-term care insurance. We were offered it back about 15 years ago and declined because we thought it was too expensive. Boy, too expensive?" She shook her head. "Look at the expense of not getting it," she mumbled to herself.

"How much was it?"

"I think we were quoted about $2,500 a year for both of us. The worst part is that the cost would have been manageable. At the time, we had more money than we needed. We rejected it on the principle of paying so much money for something we might never use. I regret that decision every day."

We were suddenly interrupted by the sound of the phone ringing. Judith slowly stood. "Excuse me, dear."

She picked up the phone and began speaking into the receiver. Something was wrong. I could hear her only faintly, but her tone was different from our conversation. "How long has it been?" "Has he eaten anything?" "Can't Meredith do anything?" Then finally, "Alright, I'll be right there."

She hung up with a distressed look. "I'm sorry Sam; I'm going to have to cut our meeting short. There is a problem with Tom and they need me at The Hamblin House right away."

"Oh, alright. Are you okay?"

"Sure, I'll be fine." Just as she finished the last word, she burst out crying. As she wept she said, "I'm so sorry that you have to see me like this. Tom isn't eating. The nurse that can usually get him to eat is on vacation, and he's putting up a fight. I usually have success with it so they want my help."

"Judith, you're in no condition to drive, let me take you."

"No, dear. I'll be fine. I will manage the way I have always managed."

"I know you can do it, but you have always been alone in the past. I know we've only just met, but you don't have to do this alone. At least for one day, let me help you."

Through tear-filled eyes she looked up at me and nodded. "Alright, Sam… alright."

She shuffled down the hall and grabbed a set of keys from a hook. "The car is in the garage. We'll go out through the kitchen."

I quickly packed up my things from the table and followed her out the door.

As I began to slip into the car it suddenly dawned on me: What was I doing? I didn't know this woman. I've never been around an Alzheimer's patient. As I put the key in the ignition, Judith grabbed my hand, looked at me and said, "Thank you so much. I really appreciate you being here with me." Immediately, any question or doubt vanished.

We spoke very little on the car ride to The Hamblin House. As we pulled into the driveway I noticed just how lovely the place was. Despite its enormous size, the architecture made it feel like home. Judith led the march to the administrator's office after being greeted by a woman at the reception desk and a large male orderly.

We stopped at an office just a few doors down from the front desk. There, a man in his mid-50's saw Judith and rushed off his phone call. His delight was genuine as he greeted her with a double-handed handshake.

"Hello Judith. Thanks for coming down so quickly. He's begun to get very irritable since he hasn't been eating for some time. We really would appreciate your help."

"Of course. I'll get the old stubborn coot to eat," she said seriously.

The man noticed me. "Who is this? Is this your granddaughter?"

"No," replied Judith. "Just a friend."

I reached out my hand to shake his. "Sam Clason, nice to meet you."

"Bob Travers. I am the director of Hamblin House. Please, follow me. We'll head down to Tom's room."

We walked through a maze of hallways until we finally arrived at a small room where Tom, looking old and frail, sat in a recliner watching television. An orderly was changing the sheets on his bed. As Judith entered, Tom stood up and said, "Thank God you're here. You need to help me. This man is an imposter. He is trying to rip me off. He has been searching through my sheets for about 10 minutes looking for loose change!"

Judith didn't respond immediately, just hugged him. "Just calm down, I'm here. Everything will be alright."

Tom looked her in the eyes. "What's your name? You're beautiful. Is there a lucky man in your life, or are you single?"

"Oh no," Judith said with a smirk, "there is a lucky man alright. I am sure if you knew him, you'd like him very much."

"I'm sure I would." Tom said as he grew noticeably less agitated and sat back in his chair. "Who is this?" he said as he motioned to me. "Is this your lovely daughter?"

"No, no," said Judith with the patience of a saint, "this is Sam; she is a friend who came to visit."

"Oh, she didn't steal my hand clock, did she? I know someone in this place stole it. Everybody in here is trying to rip me off."

What the heck is a hand clock? I thought to myself.

The orderly moved over to the nightstand drawer, opened it, pulled out a wristwatch, and handed it to Judith. "Here is his hand clock."

Judith handed it to Tom, who grabbed it and said with a scowl, "I told you they stole it."

Judith, ignoring his comment, sat down next to him on an ottoman and said, "Why aren't you eating?"

"Mother told me no snacks before dinner. So, I am waiting for dinner."

"Well, mother asked me to look after you and I made you dinner. If you eat every last bite, I promise you can have a treat."

He suddenly looked disarmed, afraid. "Mother sent you?"

"Yes, Tommy."

"Is she angry?"

"Not angry, just concerned that you haven't eaten your dinner."

"I don't want Mother to be angry. I'll eat my dinner, I promise. I'll be a good boy."

"That's fine, Tommy. I'll tell your mother you did a good job if you eat every last bite on your plate." The orderly handed Judith a tray of food, which she put in front of Tom. He looked it over, took a long sniff of it, and said, "Yum, meatloaf. Mother makes the best meatloaf."

It was indeed meatloaf, but the food looked cold and flat, obviously it had been sitting for some time. Tom didn't seem to care. He began eating as Judith stood up, rubbed his back, and hummed to him. It was perhaps one of the most beautiful and sad moments I'd ever witnessed. This was unconditional love in its purest form. Judith did not hesitate to give it so freely knowing she would receive none in return.

Tom, true to his word, devoured every morsel on his tray. His reward was two cookies Bob had brought up from the kitchen.

We spent another half-hour with Tom. Although Judith still loved her husband very much, it seemed that his condition had taken a greater toll on her than on him. The strain was undeniable. She was tired.

The way home was again quiet. The silence became uncomfortable, so I broke it.

"Judith, why did you reply to my ad? I'm not saying that it wasn't a good idea, but the financial pain seems minimal compared with the pain of watching your husband suffer the way he is."

"Definitely," she confirmed, staring out the passenger window. "But, it's tough enough to lose your husband this way; to lose your house and your sense of security along with it, that does not need to happen. It can be prevented, even if the Alzheimer's can't."

Her logic was undeniable. I decided there would be no need to ask her what this mistake had cost her. The price was painfully obvious.

Travel Notes: April 1st, 2010

Today was a difficult one. I have never experienced such a combination of heart wrenching pain and unconditional love. When a loved one is sick and their physical capacities begin to falter, it is not hard to know what to do; it is when their mental acuteness fails that creates the dilemma.

Unfortunately, although Tom's illness may have been unavoidable, the financial strains felt by Judith did not have to be. Tom and Judith could have been living comfortably had they executed the right game plan years ago. Unfortunately, this lack of action has left Judith with only regret during a period where her emotional dam is already cresting.

Chapter 13
Thomas & Latesha Gibson

With only three stops remaining, I found myself longing for home. The visits I had with the people I met on this journey were the only distraction from the growing homesickness.

The short drive from the train station to the home of Thomas and Latesha Gibson did not disappoint; Holly Springs, NC was green and warm in mid-April. Despite spending much of the past six weeks in the southern half of the country, I never grew bored of the mild temperatures.

The Gibsons' home was a treat unto itself, with marble columns and a sprawling front porch, the first plantation estate I'd seen on my trip. With the ringing of the doorbell came thunderous barking from behind enormous oak doors. "Hush up," boomed a voice from somewhere inside. Are these people really experiencing retirement difficulties? I thought to myself.

There, at the considerable opening where the door once was, stood a man sporting reading glasses and a small band of white hair that marked a semi-circle around the back of his head.

"Good afternoon, Miss Clason," the man said with a big smile.

"You must be Mr. Gibson?" I asked and held out my hand to shake his.

He shook my hand firmly and replied, "Thomas Gibson. Welcome to our home!"

I entered the house to find the perfect combination of elegance, southern charm, and comfort. The two-story foyer featuring a winding staircase with wrought-iron rail was my introduction.

"You have a beautiful home, Mr. Gibson."

"Please, call me Thomas. Thank you very much. We love it. It is our most prized possession. We built it from the ground up in 1972." He closed the door. "Follow me; Latesha is warming up some homemade crab chowder. My specialty."

We walked into a living room that had vaulted ceilings, antique furniture, and a beautiful, two-story stone fireplace. The walls were lined with bookshelves and more volumes than I had seen at most libraries.

I followed Thomas through another archway into a kitchen just about the size of my apartment, featuring granite countertops, Viking appliances, and beautifully stained and detailed mahogany cabinets. It offered no less than three eating nooks, two of which overlooked the sprawling grounds of the estate.

"Well, hello there," came a pleasant greeting from Latesha, who was standing in front of the stove. Although I knew she was in her 70's, she looked younger. Her hair was a stark white mixed with grey, and she wore a giant red apron. She walked towards me with her arm extended. "Latesha Gibson, welcome to our home."

"Samantha Clason, call me Sam. You have an amazing home. It's the nicest I have ever been in."

"You are just too kind, sweetheart. Thank you. We like it too. Can I get you something to drink?" she asked.

"Water would be great, thanks."

"Are you sure that's all you want? I just made a fresh pitcher of sweet tea. It's Thomas's favorite."

"Well, sure, I would love to try some, if it's not an imposition."

"Imposition? Please, you are our guest. It's never an imposition." She turned back towards the fridge. "I'm warming up a pot of Thomas's famous crab chowder. I hope you're hungry, but even if you're not, you have got to have a bowl. It is absolutely delicious.

Thomas has spent the last 20 years perfecting it."

"I'd love some, thank you."

"I figured we would sit over here." Thomas said, motioning towards the little living area off to the left. "This should be comfortable for everyone."

Latesha placed a tall glass of sweet tea on a coaster on the table in front of me. "So, you have been on the road, is that correct?" Thomas asked.

"Yes, for almost three months now I have been traveling across the country."

"Wow, what prompted all of this?"

"Well, first and foremost, I'm a freelance writer by trade." I told them the story of my background, my visit to Aunt Cindy, and the project. I went through a little bit about the journey so far and what I had learned. They sat and listened intently, with the exception of Latesha, who got up from time to time to stir the chowder.

"Wow," said Thomas at the end of my tale. "That is an incredible story. I wish you lots of luck when you get home. I think it could be a fantastic article. From the sound of it, you may even have a full book on your hands."

"We'll see. I've never written a book before, so I'm not sure if that's even possible."

"Don't sell yourself short, Sam. A book is just a long article. The information you are gathering is information people need, and there is enough there that one article will almost certainly not be enough. You will need at least a series of articles."

I didn't know exactly what I had yet, but I knew Thomas was right. One article would never be sufficient.

Just then, Latesha brought me over a bowl of steaming hot chowder, put it on the table in front of me, and sat herself. "Would you like some crackers, dear?" she asked.

"No thank you. This is perfect. So," I said, "I am here to learn a little about your retirement mistakes. Tell me, what's your story?"

Latesha began, "Thomas was an attorney. In fact, he was the first African American attorney to graduate from UNC Chapel Hill. After a couple of years of not being taken seriously in the corporate world, he decided to start his own practice in the early '60's. He began to make a name for himself trying civil rights cases. Obviously, this was very fertile ground in the South during the '60's. Right place, right time. He became known in North Carolina as the civil rights attorney."

"My practice had grown so large that at one point I had 31 attorneys and 45 employees working for me. We had made it." Thomas interjected.

Latesha continued, "A civil rights lawyer in the South in the '60's was a stressful and difficult career. We received death threats almost daily, and Thomas took his work very seriously."

"It wasn't just a career for me," Thomas added. "As an African-American, I was doing my part to further the Civil Rights Movement, and I was passionate about it. I could not let my clients down. I worked 80-hour weeks, nights, weekends, you name it."

"So," Latesha continued, "we always knew it made sense for Thomas to retire early. There is not a doubt in our mind that he would be in his grave now if he hadn't. At 53, he sold his practice, worked two more years as an employee for the new owner, and retired."

"Did you enjoy retirement?" I asked after swallowing a mouthful of the delicious chowder.

"Oh yes, at least at the beginning," Thomas answered. "I always loved crabbing, so I spent a lot of time doing just that. I also took up cooking, using the crab that I had caught. I learned how to make dozens of dishes out of crab. My favorite, of course, you are eating right now."

"I actually had a fair amount of savings and when I sold my practice, we agreed that the buyer would pay me over 20 years. So, we had a substantial income for some time. However, we did very little planning for when that income stopped. We never asked ourselves, 'What if we live into our 90's?' Although we live a very nice lifestyle, everything we own is paid for. The house is paid off, the cars are paid. We don't carry any debt. But I've been retired so long already, over 20 years, that we have been living off our assets a long time and there is not much left. Utilities are still expensive and since we have a lot of land, the property taxes are high as well. We've been dipping into savings for four years now since the payments from the practice have stopped, and we are almost out of money. Another year or so and we will be living strictly on Social Security."

Latesha interjected, "If we are forced to live on Social Security alone, we will not be able to afford this house. I don't want that to happen!"

"The problem is," Thomas added, "now I am too old to work. I have thought about leveraging my reputation in the civil rights field to work as a consultant, but unfortunately I have been out of the game so long, people see me as a dinosaur, a legend, more than an actual resource. I've had no luck finding any kind of consulting work."

"I only wish that instead of retiring altogether that I would have just pulled back, worked part time for another 10 years or so. I easily could have made enough to live and would have had no trouble finding consulting work at that point. That is the reason we called you. That was our big mistake. I never should have fully retired so young."

"Honestly," Thomas continued, "I also grew bored. Sure, I love crabbing and cooking, but we were never blessed with children, so we have no real family, and I started missing the intellectual stimulation of work. Although I was tired at 55, I really did enjoy the challenge and I began to miss that a few years after I retired."

"So, what is your plan for next year?" I asked.

"We really don't know. It depends on a few things, but right now we don't really have one," Latesha answered.

I asked them my usual question about why they'd decided to answer my AARP ad.

Thomas replied, "I always got the most joy out of my work, not from the money I made or the size of my firm, but the people I helped. Maybe I am just being narcissistic, but I truly believe I played an important role in the Civil Rights Movement here in the South. I miss that. I miss making a difference and helping people. This gives me the ability to help again. Let's face it; we all learn best from our mistakes. It would be a shame if people made the same mistakes over and over again because nobody was willing to talk about it. I would much rather risk embarrassment than the continuing of ignorance. Ignorance helps nobody."

"Wow, very well put," I said. "Finally, what do you think this mistake has cost you?'

Again, Thomas chimed in. "I guess that remains to be seen. As of right now, our lifestyle hasn't changed much. We still live our lives the way we did 20 years ago, with perhaps a tad more caution towards our spending. But, we will be devastated if we need to sell the house. I guess for now, it is fear. The fear of the unknown. The uncertainty of it all. In your late seventies, you don't want to worry about where your income will come from next year. You want to know that your financial situation is handled no matter what happens for the rest of your life. We don't have that luxury. I guess that is the cost now, and it could be far greater in the future."

"For me, the cost is worry," said Latesha. "I really get upset thinking about the prospect of having to move out of the house just because we can't afford the utilities, let alone the taxes. I just wish we had done a few things differently."

I realized at this point that I had eaten almost none of the chowder. I was so focused on their story that it had slipped my mind. I began eating the tasty soup as we spent some more time talking about Thomas's life as a civil rights trial attorney. I listened intently, understanding that I was learning about the Civil Rights Movement from a man who was on the front lines. This was a once in a lifetime opportunity.

Before I left, Latesha gave me a tour of the house. I was in awe. Although no room moved me as much as the kitchen, the entire house was a treasure. I could see why the thought of moving out of this amazing home they had built would be depressing.

Travel Notes: April 13th, 2010

Man was not designed to be idle. We either push forward and grow, or we begin to deteriorate towards death. Thomas retired too early. Despite the stress and pressure he felt from work, relaxation and diversion alone could not provide him happiness. This is not to say that enjoying some downtime isn't an important aspect of life; only, it shouldn't define life.

Perhaps a better solution would have been to find work doing something that stimulated his curiosity and passion without the pressure. This small distinction can often mean the difference between financial success and failure in retirement.

Chapter 14
The Return Home

Over the loudspeaker the conductor boomed, "This stop, Red Bank", as I collected my things. I was elated to be home after more than three months of a nomadic existence. The contents of my apartment remained undisturbed; I burst through the door to the smell of stale air. With the exception of opening a few windows, I was in no mood to do anything. I collapsed on my bed and stared at the ceiling.

That's when reality hit. I had spent over three months and almost $20,000 to gather the information that lay on my laptop, the recorded story of 33 individuals who were willing to share their retirement mistakes. The long journey I was in the midst of had no obvious path, and I wrestled with the question of how to proceed.

Writer's block is a phenomenon I've experienced often in my career. What I learned was that forgetting about the topic for a short period inevitably led to a breakthrough. Although I was not dealing with writer's block, I felt the solution could be applicable to the current problem. So that's what I did. A few more minutes on my bed, and I picked up the phone to call my Mom and began to unpack.

"Hello, my baby!" she answered, a bit of a song in her voice. "I take it you're home."

"Hi Mom. Yup, I got in about a half hour ago."

"I am so glad. How'd everything go? Are you glad to be home?"

"Everything went well. The trip back was fine. I'm glad to be back. Just a little overwhelmed."

"Overwhelmed! Why?"

"Well, I spent Dad's money and the last three months of my life gathering all of this information, and I haven't a clue what I'm going to do with it. Who wants to read about 33 people who messed up their retirement?"

"Well, I'm sure you will think of something, sweetie. You're very creative. You know where a good place to start may be? Talk to a financial planner. I have an advisor that your father and I had always worked with, and he is great at this stuff. Someone like that might be a good resource for you."

Why didn't I think of that? It was the much needed starting point that had evidently eluded me. "That's a great idea, Mom. I'll do that."

We chatted a little longer and said our goodbyes. Within seconds of hanging up the phone, I was at my laptop Googling financial planners in the Monmouth County area. The choices seemed endless. I spent much of the rest of the day filtering through experts with a string of letters after their names. Finally, I found who I was looking for: his name was Tyler Robertson.

Tyler works for a small boutique firm in Red Bank. He has an impressive education and experience in the field, working with those in retirement. He was my first and only phone call to a financial planner. We spoke and set an appointment to meet the following week.

Tyler greeted me in his waiting room with a firm handshake. He was relatively young and handsome, with strawberry blonde hair and piercing blue eyes. He led me back to his office, where we spent the next 45 minutes discussing the details of my project and the stories I had prepared from my trip notes.

He seemed interested and curious about what I was trying to accomplish, but cautioned me that he was a busy man and reading all the material I'd left with him would take time. I made it clear that I was in no rush.

To my surprise, Tyler called me less than a week later. His tone was hurried and excited as he asked for me to come meet him immediately. Given my somewhat clear schedule, that wasn't a problem.

"Sam, do you know what you have here?" he said, without so much as a hello.

"No, what?"

"You have the rulebook on exactly what not to do in retirement. This is incredible. I have never seen anything like this. The best part is, it's not from some guy on television or financial advisor. This is information directly from the source. These are real people who have made real mistakes."

"That's why I did it. I wanted to meet real people and hear their stories."

"You want to know something even more amazing? As I was reading the stories, I began to notice a pattern. So, each time I read a story I wrote down the mistake the retiree made in that particular tale. If I saw the same mistake twice, I just put a mark next to the mistake I had already written down. What you uncovered is that there are only seven mistakes made in all 33 cases."

"You know, I did notice a pattern when I was interviewing these people."

"I know, amazing, right? So, this morning I came in early and began going through client files, looking at my own notes of mistakes people had made before they came to work with me. Every single one of my files had a mistake that fell into the category of one of these seven. I think you have inadvertently uncovered the seven mistakes made by people in retirement."

I laughed. "You mean the seven deadly retirement sins?"

"Exactly! This is important information. Information people need. I can see the title now," he said, holding up his hands as if reading a headline, "The Seven Most Common Mistakes to Avoid in Retirement."

"Alright," I agreed, "I think you are on to something here, but how do I write it? Should it be a series of articles, a book, a blog, what?"

"Let's not put the cart before the horse. Let's write it as a series of articles. We can always go back, put them together and make a book." Tyler got up, walked around his desk and sat on the corner of it, right in front of me, with a serious look on his face. "I would really like to help you with this. You're going to need a wingman, an expert that can guide you through the financial side. I would like to be that resource. I really think this is something special and if you'll have me, I'd love to be a part of it."

"Absolutely," I replied. "I am scared to death to do this on my own. You should see my finances, they're a disaster. I wouldn't know where to start."

The next few weeks were spent hammering out the details of the partnership, and we went to work. Over six weeks I met with Tyler three times a week, each meeting lasting hours. He was a busy man in great demand who was taking a big risk investing so much of his time into the project. Fortunately, the results were well worth our efforts.

Part 3:
The 7 Deadly Retirement Sins

Chapter 15
Sin #1: Retiring too early or living above your means

"People do not lack strength, they lack will"
- **Victor Hugo**

Retirement is a strange time of life. It is the point when we decide that the life we have been building and working towards will now change dramatically. It is the intention of every retiree that their lives will change for the better; however, no matter the intention, it is not always the case.

Many find themselves bored in retirement, physically and mentally unchallenged. As Dr. Victor Frankl stated in Man's Search for Meaning, "What man actually needs is not a tensionless state, but rather the striving and struggling for a worthwhile goal, a freely chosen task." It is not uncommon for retirees to enjoy their first few months or even years of freedom from the daily drudgery of work, only to feel unfulfilled and unhappy once the initial "honeymoon" wears off. Obviously, this is different for everyone; some retirees relish their new found freedom.

However, the threat to your happiness in retirement is both emotional and financial.

Retiring too early and living above your means may appear at first blush to be different problems, but the end result is the same. When one shortens their working years and thus their income and savings, they create a larger need for the resources that are intended to support their retirement.

This is true of living above your means in retirement. If one has the ability to comfortably draw $40,000 per year from their portfolio and they decide instead to draw $70,000, they are putting far too much pressure on their financial reservoir. Almost inevitably, this will lead to a drying up of funds as the retiree ages, when those funds are the most crucial.

Sin #1 is running out of money at a time when it would be the most detrimental. When the retiree is in their 80's and even 90's, there is a very good chance that they will no longer possess the ability to work, leaving few options.

On my journey cross-country, I met with 33 retirees who had all made retirement mistakes. Of those 33 individuals and couples, a full quarter of them had made a mistake that fell into this category. It is obviously a common problem.

The Gibsons of Holly Springs, NC are the quintessential example of this first sin. Thomas had a very successful and lucrative career as an attorney. Their beautiful house, fine furnishings, and high lifestyle were evidence that money had not been a concern. However, Thomas decided to retire at the relatively early age of 55 - certainly not impossible, but it put a financial strain on their resources. The Gibsons are now unable to work and left with few options.

Let's look at a simple analysis of retirement at three different ages for Jane Dow, who is making $60,000 a year and has $500,000 saved heading into age 62. We will explore the options of retirement for Jane at ages, 62, 66, and 70.

Retirement Options for Jane Dow			
Retirement Age	62	66	70
Years Retired	28	24	20
ASSETS			
Investments	$500,000	$708,680	$982,210
INCOME			
Social Security	$14,400	$19,152	$26,121
Portfolio income	$41,195	$61,789	$92,713
Annual Income	$55,595	$80,941	$118,834
Assumptions: 7% rate of return on investments, Full Retirement Age for Social Security is 66, age of death age 90			

As you can see from the chart above, waiting a mere four years can increase your annual income in retirement by more than 45%. Waiting eight years can increase your annual income by over 100%. Why such a dramatic difference?

Even forgoing retirement one additional year increases both sides of the balance sheet, and dramatically alters income options. The benefits include:

Your investment portfolio has one more year of undisturbed growth: It is perhaps the largest year of growth since the power of compounding provides the last years of growth to be the greatest.

You have one less year of retirement: If you are planning retirement through age 90, retiring at 66 means one less year your assets must support you.

One additional year of savings: During perhaps the highest earning period of your life when your expenses may be very low due to a paid off mortgage or no children to provide for, this one additional year of savings can prove very advantageous.

An increase in Social Security income: Delaying Social Security even one year can add as much as 8% to your monthly benefit. Social Security is often the best source of income you can receive in retirement, due to its tax efficiency, cost of living adjustment, and government guarantee. These benefits create a strong incentive to maximize it for later life.

If delaying retirement one year can add all of these benefits, think about the power of delaying four or eight years. It can have a dramatic improve your retirement lifestyle.

Obviously, all of the positives we are analyzing are strictly financial. There are many non-monetary benefits to retiring early. Spending more time with your family, pursuing hobbies, charitable interests, and travel are all worthwhile and noble pursuits. However, how much time is needed to accomplish these pursuits? What is the cost if retirement is attempted too early? It inevitably affects the retiree late in life when earning income is no longer a viable option.

Thomas Gibson is well educated and experienced. Even if the daily grind and stress of running his practice proved too much, he had many options working part time in a far less stressful environment. Once retirement came at age 55, he could have worked as a consultant, continued at his old firm part-time, or even done something completely different that he enjoyed and provided him income. Remaining at work to some extent would have furnished the Gibson's additional earned income and kept Thomas mentally and physically stimulated, with minimal stress. His mistake may not have been retiring too early, but the complete cessation of all earned income.

Living above your means in retirement can create a very similar problem to the one faced by the Gibsons. This problem has less to do with timing, but the management of the resources you have. The example that best demonstrates this mistake is my good friend Mary Dement of San Diego. Mary lived a very nice life in her retirement with her husband Howard. They traveled, stayed at the finest hotels, ate at the nicest restaurants, and bought expensive gifts for their grandchildren. Living the retirement most of us only dream of in their early retirement years. However, now that Howard has passed away Mary is paying a very dear price for their decadent lifestyle.

Despite the warnings by their financial advisor time and again, Howard and Mary lived beyond their means and burned quickly through their retirement savings. This has furnished Mary with few options. The sale of her beautiful home is the only viable choice. At 84, with no family nearby, this is a very daunting and undesirable task.

Many retirees head into retirement with a mentality that they will not want for anything. It is often said by such individuals, "I have worked hard all of my life and I deserve this!" Much as a teenager leaving the comfort of Mom and Dad's house for the first time and heading off to the cruel harsh world, new retirees often have a sense of entitlement. They feel that since they have put in 40 years or more of hard work, they can have and do whatever it is they want in retirement. It is their right.

By the time they learn of their faulty assumption, it is too late. Unfortunately, there is no direct correlation between the intensity of work and your comfort in retirement. It does not matter what you think you deserve or are entitled to; what matters is what you have saved, the assets and income sources you have established. These two aspects alone will determine what you can live on. Your arbitrary idea of what you deserve matters little.

In Howard and Mary's case, they knew exactly what they could live on. They worked with a financial planner who developed an income level that would provide them with a long comfortable retirement. Their problem was that they simply ignored it and overspent. This overspending quickly cannibalized their portfolio, and left Mary with few alternatives to selling her house. Now, at 84, she has essentially lost her ability to go back to work. She is now forced to cut costs, something she could have done voluntarily a few years earlier when it would have allowed her to stay in her house.

Solution: There are numerous options to avoid being affected by Sin #1. Let's explore them.

- **Know what you can spend:** No matter how long your retirement is, if you live at or below your means, you have very little chance of running out of money. Work with a fee-only financial professional who can help you develop a plan for your retirement spending. Once you have a number that works, stick to it. Don't get caught up in the "I deserve this" mentality. You deserve a long and comfortable retirement. No cruise or set of golf clubs is worth risking that.

- **Delay retirement as long as possible:** I do not want to dash the hopes of any would-be retirees out there who were pining to retire at a young age; however, as we've seen in this chapter, it is generally financially advisable to delay retirement. Delaying retirement will provide you with a better long-term quality of life and the peace of mind that your later years are far more likely to be financially secure. Obviously, this is specific to your circumstances and another area where a good financial planner can help.

- **Get a part-time job:** Working part-time when you retire is a perfect segue into retirement bliss. Find a job where you are paid well to utilize your natural talents doing something you love, and it won't even feel like work. If this is available to you 2-3 days a week, you may be able to avoid touching your nest egg (which will then continue to grow undisturbed) and you will remain stimulated mentally, physically, and socially while taking much of the stress of the daily grind out of your life. Work when you are able to, so you are not backed into a corner in late retirement when work is no longer an option.

Chapter 16
Sin #2: Improper Investment Asset Allocation

*"Only when the tide goes out do you discover
who's been swimming naked."*
- **Warren Buffett**

How your money is managed in retirement is almost as important as how much you have to manage. Previous generations were not burdened with the challenge faced by retirees today. In the past, an employee retired from the company they had labored with for their entire career to the rewards of a pension, health insurance, and even a gold watch!

But the dependence on your employer to provide for your retirement is an antiquated notion. The 401k and IRA have replaced pensions and annuities as the retirement vehicles of the modern era. Although there are many positive aspects to this new kind of financial self-reliance, the obvious negative is that someone with little or no knowledge or experience in the area of finance has the responsibility of managing their own investments. This shift has been painful for many.

The sin of improper asset allocation was committed by no less than 15 of the 33 people I met on my trip - by far the most common error.

Three Portfolio Killers in Retirement

Essentially, there are only three threats to your retirement portfolio that can lead to Sin #2. The reason they are committed so often is they tend to be in conflict with each other. The novice investor has a tendency to manage one risk by inadvertently accepting another, often leading to poor results.

It is vital that all three are understood and managed to properly avoid succumbing to Sin #2:

1. Over-Concentration:

If all of your eggs are in one basket, what happens if you (or somebody else) drops the basket? Over-concentration is the risk that investors subject themselves to by owning too much of any one investment.

Over-concentration can occur in many forms. It is most often demonstrated when an investor holds too much of a single stock, bond, or other investment. Let's reflect on the Abernathes to demonstrate the danger of this type of over-concentration.

Jon Abernathe was brought up knowing nothing but General Motors. The company had provided for his family for generations. He had faith in GM even after its total collapse.

The Abernathes felt the sharp sting of over-concentration when their only investment, General Motors, filed for bankruptcy. The troubles that plagued this one company in turn plagued their retirement.

It may seem difficult to imagine poor performance or even bankruptcy for gigantic companies like Coca-Cola, Proctor & Gamble, or Exxon Mobile, but it happens. Consider the fact that there is only one company remaining in the Dow Jones Industrial Average from 100 years ago. All 30 companies in the Dow in 1911 were the largest blue-chip companies of their day. Times change, consumers' tastes evolve, and products become obsolete. Even the best companies eventually become extinct.

It is common for investors to become emotionally tied to an investment. This phenomenon is often seen in employees who own their company's stock, those who inherit stock from a deceased relative, or an individual who has had a good track record investing with a single company and mistakenly think they "owe" that company their allegiance. Whatever the reason, over-concentration is almost never logical; it's emotional. The investor feels a certain loyalty to the company that tends to blind them to the risks of their over-concentration.

In the case of the Abernathes, it was their blind faith in GM that caused them to overlook the tremendous risk they were accepting. Regardless of whether they understood it, they tied their future to the fate of General Motors - with disastrous consequences.

It may not have seemed risky to the Abernathes. After all, GM was a blue-chip stock and one of the leaders in a mature industry. The company had been around almost 100 years, and had done well for previous generations. Unfortunately, the truth is that we live in a dynamic age where business changes rapidly. GM, like all companies, was at the mercy of any number of potential problems: poor management, a catastrophic event such as a lawsuit, or antiquated products, just to name a few. Despite GM's track record, they were nothing more than one company that, as we saw, was not infallible.

The successful investor understands that it is important to think logically, not emotionally, when managing their investments. In the case of the employee who holds too much company stock, they may not understand that their income is already tied to the firm. Is it logical to tie their investments as well? Consider the cases of Enron (one of the largest energy distributors in the world) and WorldCom (one of the largest communications companies in the world) where employees lost not only their jobs, but also their 401ks or investments that were tied to the stock. In these cases, many employees were hit by a double financial whammy that would be very difficult to overcome.

In the case of inheritance, it is important to remember that your deceased relative left the money to you to enjoy. This asset is now yours to do with as you see fit. Do not feel obligated to do what your relative "would have wanted." If you were to end up destitute in retirement, your deceased relative would not be there to pick up the pieces. You are the only one that can make decisions based on your assets, and you should never feel beholden to the memory of a long-deceased relative to make those decisions.

Finally, there is the case of the investor who feels loyal to a specific company or investment that has provided positive returns in the past. Loyalty to what? Companies and stocks are not living, breathing organisms. They are investment vehicles. Although you may have an affinity for a corporate mission or a certain CEO, the point of your investing should always be to maximize your return. Just because a company has done well for you in the past does not mean it is likely to continue to do well. Loyalty due to outperformance often leads to underperformance.

Your decisions affect your future. You must take the responsibility to decide what is best.

Over-concentration can be specific to an entire industry as well. Often, when one company is going through a difficult time, the entire industry feels the effect. This was evident during the technology bust of 2001 as well as the financial crisis of 2008/2009. If the Abernathes had invested half of their money with GM and the other half with Ford, they may not have lost everything; but they would not have saved much as Ford shares fell over 90% during the same difficult stretch. Diversifying their GM investment with Ford stock would have been a poor strategy.

Over-concentration isn't applicable only to stocks. If you used your life savings to buy a piece of beachfront property only to watch it be destroyed by a hurricane, you would have experienced firsthand an over-concentration in real estate. The same is true for purchasing a large bond from a bond issuer who can no longer make payments on their bond and defaults.

Investing all or most of our money in one company, investment, or asset class is a gamble that can have dire consequences to our financial future.

2. Inflation

Inflation is defined simply as the gradual increase in prices of the goods and services we use every day, and is the often-overlooked silent killer of a comfortable and happy retirement. How much did it cost to go to a movie 30 years ago? What was the cost of a gallon of gas, or a postage stamp?

Over time, prices tend to increase. This is the fundamental nature of inflation. What we pay today in property taxes is probably only a fraction of what we will pay in the future. Using history as a guide, we can expect a 3.5 - 4% increase in prices, on average, each year. This means that if it costs $1 today to buy a Coke, and inflation grows at 4% per year on a compounded basis, the cost of your Coke will be $1.48 in 10 years - an increase of almost 50%. In 30 years, that same Coke will cost $3.24.

What happens to your $1 if you put it under the mattress today? Next year, you can no longer afford a Coke. In fact, every year you keep your money under the mattress, the Coke gets further and further out of reach. The actual dollar hasn't changed, but its value has. Your dollar becomes worth less and less with the passage of time.

However, let's say you choose to take your dollar out from under the mattress and invest it with the expectation of gaining a return. If the cost of your Coke is growing at 4% per year and your return on investment is 3% per year, each year you are losing value to inflation. The loss in value will not be as much as if your money was under the mattress, but the return is not keeping pace with the increase. In 10 years when your Coke costs $1.48, your dollar will be worth $1.34. Better than under the mattress, but the Coke is still getting further out of reach with the passage of time.

But, what if you were able to invest and earn a return of 7% per year? As the price of your Coke increases, your investment not only grows with it, but you are actually creating additional value to purchase other things. In 10 years, when you want to purchase a Coke for $1.48, your $1 investment will now be worth $1.96. This will allow you to make your purchase and have $.48 left over.

This simple example demonstrates that your investments not only have to keep pace with inflation, but actually grow beyond it. Let's take a look at a few other costs you may be interested in:

Expense	Today's Cost	Cost In 10 Years*
Property Taxes	$4,000	$5,920.98
Gallon of Gas	$2.80	$4.14
Gallon of Milk	$4.00	$5.92
Doctor's Co-Pay	$20	$29.60
Stamp	$0.44	$0.65
*Assumes 4% inflation		

The above chart demonstrates that a mere 4% increase in prices each year will create the need for almost 50% more income in 10 years to maintain the same lifestyle. When you retire, it is vital that you prepare for this inevitable increase in prices. The first step is recognizing it exists and understanding that even "risk-free" investments, which pay low returns but carry a guarantee, usually are the most susceptible to inflation risk. There is no such thing as "risk-free." You are either going to accept some sort of portfolio volatility, or some sort of decline in purchasing power. It is up to you to decide which.

The Espinozas demonstrated the opposite extreme than the Abernathes in this second sin. Julio and Maria were poor investors who allowed fear to dictate their investment philosophy. They invested their hard-earned money only in assets that offered some type of guarantee. Bank and insurance products like CD's, money market accounts, and fixed annuities may have furnished a sound night's sleep due to security of principal, but the guarantee cost them dearly - in investments that were losing ground to the increasing costs of goods and services in retirement. Inflation was winning. The only remaining solution for the couple was to cut their wants so they could support their needs.

3. Market Fluctuations:

Market fluctuations are the last and perhaps most feared of all portfolio risks. In the age of real-time information and instant data, it is difficult for any retiree to see their account balances fall daily or even hourly. Their emotional reaction is to sell, which gets most investors into trouble.

History demonstrates that the market has consistently rewarded those who have bought into market declines and held for the long term. Declines have always been temporary, while increases have been permanent.

Thus, these price fluctuations can be a positive force for young investors who are working to accumulate assets. It allows the consistent investor to buy more shares when the stock price is low, and less shares when it's high. Over an investing lifetime it brings down the average cost per share, thus furnishing a higher return. This concept, known as dollar-cost averaging, naturally creates a buy-low, sell-high situation for the accumulating investor.

Look at this simple example of the power of volatility for an investor in the accumulation stage of investing:

Month	Money to Invest	Fund Share Price	Shares Purchased	Total Shares
1	$100	$10	10	10
2	$100	$5	20	30
3	$100	$7.5	13.33	43.33
	Total Shares	43.33		
	Total Investment	$300		
	Total Value at Month 3	$325	(43.33 shares X $7.5 per share)	
	Return	8.3%		
	Annualized Return	33.3%		

Notice how the three-month return was over 8% ($300 investment now worth $325), a tremendous personal return for an investment in which the fund is actually down 25% from where we started investing (The fund was $10 when the first purchase was made but only $7.50 by month three). The key is consistency, continuing to invest when prices fall - especially when they fall. What would the return be for the astute investor who doubled their monthly investment to $200 in month 2, when the fund cost $5 per share? The answer is a whopping 18.75%. What kind of return would the scared investor have seen if he had stopped investing when the fund fell to $5 a share? -12.5%.

As powerful as market fluctuations is as a tool for accumulating assets, that is how detrimental it is to the retiree who is living off their assets. Distribution of assets from an investment account is the opposite of accumulation. It makes sense, doesn't it? You are no longer contributing, but withdrawing from the account. Usually the sale of assets is required to raise the money to make the appropriate withdrawal. The problem for the retiree is if asset values fall in the short term. They will need to sell more of the stock to raise the same amount of money as they did previously, when the stock was higher. This creates a scenario where more stock is sold when the price is low than when high, which is not an optimal scenario for an investor. See the table below:

Table A: Highly Volatile Fund

Month	Required Monthly Withdrawal	Fund Share Price	Shares Sold	Total Shares
				1000
1	$1,000	10	100	900
2	$1,000	5	200	700
3	$1,000	7.5	133.33	566.67
4	$1,000	12.5	80.00	486.67
	Total Shares Sold	513.33		
	Remaining Value	$6,083		

Table B: Less Volatile Fund

Month	Required Withdrawal	Fund Share Price	Shares Sold	Total Shares
				1000
1	$1,000	10	100	900
2	$1,000	9	111.11	788.8889
3	$1,000	10	100.00	688.8889
4	$1,000	11	90.91	597.9798
	Total Shares Sold	402.02		
	Remaining Value	$6,578		

The fund in Table A furnished a 25% return over the entire period, while the fund in Table B returned only 10% in the same period. However, due to the fact that the fund in Table B was less volatile during those four months, the retiree had to sell only 402 shares vs. 513 in Table A. Also, the account value in Table B is worth almost $500 more than that in Table A, despite the lower fund value. This demonstrates that although the overall performance of the investment is important, it is the volatility of the portfolio being drawn from that has a substantial impact on the results for the individual investor. Remember, it's not about what the investment returns; it's about what you return.

The examples above should underscore the importance of keeping volatility to a minimum in a retiree's portfolio. Ideally, we would prefer zero volatility. However, investments that can provide zero volatility are saddled with the inability to keep up with inflation. As I mentioned earlier in this chapter, the mistake made by many retirees is avoiding the third portfolio mistake by accepting the second. Like most paradoxes in life, the solution is a simple compromise.

Solution:

It may seem impossible to provide one solution to over-concentration, inflation concerns, and high volatility. But, my guess is the solution is probably not that foreign to you.

The remedy to all of these problems is simply diversification - a financial buzzword used often by experts and non-experts alike. Despite the fact that you've heard the word before, you may not be sure exactly what it means.

Tyler defines diversification to his clients this way: "You never own enough of one asset to make a killing at it or to get killed by it." If Jon and Florence Abernathe had lived by this philosophy and had only 10% of their investments in GM stock, when the company went bankrupt they would have been able to withstand the mild shock to their portfolio with little effect on their lifestyle. Due to their lack of diversification, that is not the case. Julio and Maria Espinoza would certainly have a much larger cache and no problems maintaining their current lifestyle despite inflation if they had diversified their investments not only when they were younger, but in retirement as well.

In order to be properly diversified, the investor must begin by removing over-concentration in one or more investments. Start by taking a hard look at your portfolio. If any one company or entity went out of business or defaulted on returning your principle, how detrimental would it be to your overall return? This is not to say you shouldn't own any individual stocks or bonds; but keep each asset to no more than 5-10% of your portfolio. This will prevent a total collapse of your future if that company were to fall on hard times for an extended period, or worse, go out of business.

This theory is true for all asset classes, not just stocks. If you have bonds, try to hold many different issues from various issuers. If real estate is your game, take a hard look at your exposure if one property were to fall dramatically in value or be destroyed all together. If you have multiple properties, are they all in the same town or even the same street? What would happen to your net worth if that town or street were to become an undesirable place to live?

Look for mutual funds or ETFs (Exchange Traded Funds) that are made up of hundreds, even thousands of assets. This will ensure that if one company or asset were to go belly up, the rest of your retirement doesn't follow.

The best part of these investments is there are funds that can invest in almost anything you wish. It is easy to find funds that invest in stocks, bonds, real estate, and commodities. The broader the fund, the more diversification you maintain.

Once you are comfortable that no one company or asset can destroy your net worth, evaluate your asset classes. Asset classes are the broad investments. An example of an asset class is cash, bonds, or small-cap stocks. It is common to see retirees with 100% of their portfolio in cash (like the Espinozas), stocks, bonds, or real estate. An investor falls in love with one asset class and although they no longer have single-stock risk, it is possible to see a single asset class fall 80-90%. What if you have all real estate holdings and real estate falls 40% nationwide? What if you used all your money to buy bonds at 4% and rates rise to 8%, making your 4% bonds worth far less? Although there would be little fear of your portfolio ending up worthless, these dramatic swings can be far too difficult to bear.

Most often, the reason for over-concentration in a particular asset class is the mistaken assumption that an investor has the ability to predict the future. This is why most people, even money managers, fail at investing. It is perhaps the single greatest myth perpetrated on the American public about investing and once you understand and acknowledge it, it will change your investing life. The message is simply this: Nobody can predict the future movements of stocks, bonds, interest rates, or the economy with any level of consistency. It is sheer folly to think otherwise.

The best money managers in the world (Warren Buffett, Peter Lynch, and George Soros) are not successful because they are better at predicting the future than others. They are successful because they are better at profiting from the average investor's greed and fear. These fantastic money managers know that when the average investor is selling his stocks after they have fallen 60% because he is scared to lose all his money, that is the best time to pick up bargains. They are buying a dollar's worth of assets for $.40, and they don't care if it takes the general public 2, 5, even 10 years to recognize its true value. Bargain hunting for solid investments is a lucrative business.

The opposite is also true. When Joe Q. Public is out purchasing stocks at inflated prices because they went up 100% last year and Joe wants to get in on the action, smart managers are selling their assets to Joe. Why? Because now Joe is paying $1.50 for something worth a dollar. In order to buy low and sell high, you must always do the exact opposite of what everyone else is doing. This may seem like common sense, but common sense is not common in the investing world.

Great investors are not proactive; counter to popular opinion, they're reactive. A sailor doesn't jump in his boat, set his sail, and hope the wind blows the right way. Great investors wait to see which way the wind is blowing, then set their sail accordingly to get where they need to go.

Studies have shown time and again that those who have tried to predict future stock prices and economic trends were met with serious underperformance. Don't make this mistake with your retirement. Don't bet your future on your opinion of where things will be tomorrow. You do not know with any level of certainty where interest rates will be next year, where the Dow Jones Industrial Average will be next month, or where the price of Apple will be next week. Hot trends and fads come and go. If a sector or a stock is hot or the wave of the future, it is probably already overvalued. Accept this as fact, and you will finally be able to have some consistent growth in your portfolio.

If you agree with your inability to predict the future move of an asset class, then what do you invest in? The answer is obvious: everything. A portfolio that contains stocks, bonds, real estate, commodities, and cash not only has far less violent fluctuations, but it gives you the added advantage of rebalancing, which forces you to buy low and sell high. We will discuss rebalancing shortly.

All of the asset classes described above move somewhat independently of each other. Traditionally, when stocks rise in price, bonds fall, and vice versa. Real estate and commodities march to the beat of their own drummer; if the stock market falls, there is a good chance real estate or commodity prices will not decline.

If we had a simple portfolio of half stocks and half bonds, and the market fell 20% but bonds rose in price 10%, the total portfolio would only lose 5%. By adding real estate, commodities, and cash into the mix, we can possibly reduce fluctuations even more.

Let's assume that when you were a teenager, you worked in your eccentric uncle's hardware store. Your uncle wanted to help you start to save for retirement, and told you to set aside 5% of your salary every year. Then, at the end of each year, he will flip a coin. If the coin comes up heads, he will match 30% of everything you have saved. If it comes up tails, he will take away 10%.

The average return you can expect from your crazy uncle over time is roughly 10%. However, you run the risk of a bad series of flips. What if your uncle flipped tails for five years in a row? It is unlikely, but possible. You would be left with a poor return for five years despite the high average expected return. This may not be a risk we would like to take with our hard-earned savings.

So, you decide to suggest to your uncle that each year he split your retirement account into five parts and flip the coin five times a year. Your uncle agrees. Now, you have diversified your portfolio. Some years will certainly be better than others, but because there is now far less of a chance that 25 tails will come up in a row, you can expect a higher probability of coming closer to our expected 10% return. This is the essence of diversification.

Portfolios

You may be wondering, what is the best diversification for me given my goals, age, and risk tolerance? Developing a one-size-fits-all portfolio is difficult, dare I say impossible. Each portfolio should be customized to the individual, taking into account age, net worth, risk tolerance, and need. I strongly encourage you to seek a fee-only planner that can help you create a portfolio tailored to your specific needs. The cost will be well worth the value received. However, a templated portfolio is better than no portfolio at all. So, for demonstration purposes, Tyler has developed a series of portfolios that can be used in varying circumstances. However, please understand that I cannot stress enough the importance of a custom portfolio designed by a professional for your particular needs.

Age 50-59

Aggressive		
Symbol	**Asset Class**	**Percentage**
	Cash	5%
BND	Total Bond Index	15%
BWX	International Bond Index	10%
VNQ	Real Estate	10%
DBC	Commodities	5%
VEU	World ex. US	15%
VSS	International Small Cap	5%
VTV	Large Cap Value	15%
QQQ	Large Cap Growth	15%
VB	Small Cap Index	10%

Moderate		
Symbol	Asset Class	Percentage
	Cash	5%
SHY	Short-Term Treasuries	5%
BND	Total Bond Index	15%
BWX	International Bond Index	10%
VNQ	Real Estate	10%
DBC	Commodities	5%
VEU	World ex. US	15%
VSS	International Small Cap	5%
VTV	Large Cap Value	15%
QQQ	Large Cap Growth	10%
VB	Small Cap Index	10%

Age 50-59 *(continued)*

Conservative		
Symbol	Asset Class	Percentage
	Cash	10%
SHY	Short-Term Treasuries	10%
BND	Total Bond Index	20%
BWX	International Bond Index	10%
VNQ	Real Estate	10%
DBC	Commodities	5%
VEU	World ex. US	15%
VTV	Large Cap Value	15%
QQQ	Large Cap Growth	15%
VB	Small Cap Index	10%

Age 60-69

Aggressive		
Symbol	Asset Class	Percentage
	Cash	10%
SHY	Short-Term Treasuries	5%
BND	Total Bond Index	15%
BWX	International Bond Index	10%
VNQ	Real Estate	10%
DBC	Commodities	5%
VEU	World ex. US	10%
VSS	International Small Cap	5%
VTV	Large Cap Value	15%
QQQ	Large Cap Growth	10%
VB	Small Cap Index	5%

Age 60-69 *(continued)*

Moderate		
Symbol	Asset Class	Percentage
	Cash	10%
SHY	Short-Term Treasuries	10%
BND	Total Bond Index	20%
BWX	International Bond Index	10%
VNQ	Real Estate	10%
DBC	Commodities	5%
VEU	World ex. US	10%
VTV	Large Cap Value	10%
QQQ	Large Cap Growth	10%
VB	Small Cap Index	5%

Conservative		
Symbol	Asset Class	Percentage
	Cash	15%
SHY	Short-Term Treasuries	10%
BND	Total Bond Index	20%
BWX	International Bond Index	10%
VNQ	Real Estate	5%
DBC	Commodities	5%
VEU	World ex. US	10%
VTV	Large Cap Value	10%
QQQ	Large Cap Growth	10%
VB	Small Cap Index	5%

Age 70+

Aggressive		
Symbol	Asset Class	Percentage
	Cash	10%
SHY	Short-Term Treasuries	10%
BND	Total Bond Index	20%
BWX	International Bond Index	10%
VNQ	Real Estate	10%
DBC	Commodities	5%
VEU	World ex. US	10%
VTV	Large Cap Value	10%
QQQ	Large Cap Growth	10%
VB	Small Cap Index	5%

Moderate		
Symbol	Asset Class	Percentage
	Cash	15%
SHY	Short-Term Treasuries	10%
BND	Total Bond Index	20%
BWX	International Bond Index	10%
VNQ	Real Estate	5%
DBC	Commodities	5%
VEU	World ex. US	10%
VTV	Large Cap Value	10%
QQQ	Large Cap Growth	10%
VB	Small Cap Index	5%

Conservative		
Symbol	Asset Class	Percentage
	Cash	15%
SHY	Short-Term Treasuries	15%
BND	Total Bond Index	20%
BWX	International Bond Index	10%
VNQ	Real Estate	5%
DBC	Commodities	5%
VEU	World ex. US	10%
VTV	Large Cap Value	10%
QQQ	Large Cap Growth	10%

Each of the portfolios above will help you avoid the major retirement risks of over-concentration, inflation, and volatility. The examples use low-cost ETFs that will keep expenses low and provide broad diversification. If you would prefer no-load index mutual funds (funds that have no sales charges and track an index, thus keeping costs low) such as those offered by Vanguard, that would be an acceptable alternative.

The symbols provided in the sample portfolio are Exchange Traded Funds that are favorable for this strategy as of this writing. This will most likely change with time. The financial world is constantly improving its products and by the time you read this, there may be a better fund to accomplish these goals. Look for index funds or ETFs with low costs and broad diversification in the area you would like to invest in. Any product that meets these requirements should fulfill your needs.

Rebalancing

Rebalancing is the act of selling what has performed well in the portfolio and buying what has done poorly to return the asset allocation to its original percentages. Let's look at a simple example. Assume you had a portfolio of 50% stocks and 50% bonds. Now assume that stocks had a good year and bonds a poor year. On December 31, the portfolio has been altered due to the performances of the different asset classes to 60% stocks and 40% bonds. Your allocation of stocks and bonds is no longer where you had originally intended. The solution is a rebalance of the portfolio to bring the percentages back into an acceptable range.

In order to return the portfolio to its original allocation, you would sell off enough of the stocks and purchase enough of the bonds to return the portfolio to its desired 50/50 allocation. The additional benefit of this rebalance is that it forces the investor to buy what has done poorly and is thus cheap, and sell what has performed well and is thus expensive. Rebalancing is a mandate to buy low and sell high.

I know this may sound logical and simple to do, but I think you'll find it is a difficult task when emotions get involved. It can be unnerving in the middle of a market collapse to sell bonds that have been performing well or commodities that just increased in value 40% this year and purchase stocks that are the bane of the financial world. When stocks are down, especially during severe declines, the press trashes them. However, that is precisely why you need to sell some of the favored asset and buy the one out of vogue.

I recommend rebalancing your portfolio 1-2 times a year, depending on how volatile the assets are. Regular rebalancing has been shown to add an additional 1% or more in annual return.

Avoiding Sin #2 is not as hard as you may think. With a little common sense and recognizing the triple threat of over-concentration, inflation, and market fluctuations, the average retiree can use diversification and regular rebalancing to avoid a future similar to the Abernathes' or Espinozas'.

Chapter 17
Sin #3: Collecting Social Security at the wrong time

"I care about our young people, and I wish them great success, because they are our Hope for the Future, and some day, when my generation retires, they will have to pay us trillions of dollars in Social Security"
- Dave Barry

The Social Security Act was signed into law by Franklin D. Roosevelt in 1935. It was designed as a system of insurance to guarantee that workers would not find themselves destitute in their old age when they no longer have the capacity to work.

Social Security provides eligible citizens with a monthly income that can be helpful in retirement. Although this should be a simple system of retirement benefits, government programs rarely are. In fact, Social Security has so many subtle complexities that most retirees don't know where to start and how to manage their benefits. The retiree often suffers from analysis paralysis, and falls back on taking the benefit as soon as they become eligible. As I will attempt to demonstrate, this often leads to unwanted consequences.

Elmer Braun of Monroe, NY is an example of the consequences of Sin #3. Having collected his benefit for well over 20 years now, he recognizes the power of Social Security income. He also recognizes the mistake he made in minimizing it.

Elmer and his wife did what most Americans do when they become eligible for Social Security retirement benefits: they collected immediately. The prospect of free money from the government is too tempting for most people to delay. Without hesitation or calculation, they listen to less than sage advice from family or friends and jump at their benefit as soon as they become eligible.

This may sound like a logical move, until you understand that by collecting Social Security benefits early, those benefits are permanently reduced over the remainder of your life.

If the Brauns had decided to delay collecting their Social Security income, their benefits would have grown until he reached age 70. A larger benefit may not seem like much in early retirement, but it can be substantial later in life. This is why the decision of when to collect Social Security benefits should not be made hastily and is rarely simple.

It is not my intention to delve into the complexities of the Social Security program or attempt to educate you on the minutiae of its guidelines. However, I will give you a Cliff's Notes version of how your benefit works so you may understand why it is so important to decide wisely.

All workers who are eligible for Social Security can collect at their "Full Retirement Age," which is different for each individual depending on the year of birth. Under current law, "Full Retirement Age" can range from age 65-67. Once you reach "Full Retirement Age," you are eligible to collect your full benefit as calculated by the Social Security Administration.

However, each eligible worker may instead collect a Social Security benefit at age 62 that is reduced by anywhere from 20-30% over his or her lifetime depending on "Full Retirement Age." This means that if you begin collecting at age 62 and you would have received $2,000 per month at "Full Retirement Age," you will only collect $1,400 per month for the rest of your life - even if you live to see your 100th birthday.

The opposite is also true: If you delay your Social Security benefit past your "Full Retirement Age," your benefit will increase

8% per year until age 70. At this point, there will be no annual increases. (It is never advisable to delay Social Security past age 70 since the benefit no longer grows past this point)

If you are married, either spouse is eligible to collect their own benefit or half the benefit of their spouse, whichever is larger. Either spouse is eligible for this 50% spousal benefit regardless of whether they are eligible for their own Social Security benefit. In addition, if the spouse with the larger monthly check passes away first, the living spouse receives that larger benefit and no longer receives their smaller benefit.

Example: If John worked for 45 years, he would be eligible for his own benefit of $2,000 a month. Although his wife Rebecca never earned income and therefore is not eligible for her own benefit, she would be eligible for half of his benefit, or $1,000 per month. Their combined monthly benefit thus would equal $3,000 per month. However, if John passed away first, Mary would then be eligible for his benefit and lose hers, cutting the household income from $3,000 to $2,000 per month.

Now that you have a basic understanding of some of the complexities of Social Security that might affect your decision, let's discuss the problem with collecting at the wrong time. Fortunately, there are only two possible mistakes you can make when it comes to Social Security:

Collecting too late and dying younger than you anticipated.

Collecting too early and living longer than expected.

Although there are only two mistakes that can be made, including a spouse can complicate the decision making process. For the sake of simplicity, we will begin our discussion as if there were no spouse. Then, later, we will add some points to consider if you have a spouse.

If we evaluate the two options at first blush, where do we inherently find more risk? I think the obvious answer is in option #2. It should be apparent that we really would not see it as a tremendous financial loss if we died in our late 60s or early 70s without collecting all of the Social Security that we might have if we had lived longer. Although tragic, if you are dead, you won't care. However, I think we can all agree that being in our mid-80s and not having enough income to cover our day-to-day living expenses is a far scarier financial position.

Retirees must get away from the notion of trying to collect Social Security before it's too late. Unless we enter our 60s in poor health or have a definitive family history of premature death, it is impossible to predict the date of our demise. The average 65-year-old has a 62% chance of living to age 80. The desire for "free money" creates a temptation during a time when we should not be gambling with our finances.

Social Security should be viewed as an insurance program as was the original intent of its framers. If you begin to see Social Security as your insurance against extreme old age, you will see the importance of utilizing it for that purpose.

It is not important in most cases that we suck every dime possible out of the Social Security program. If you instead view your Social Security benefits as just one more tool in your retirement toolbox, you can begin to see the power that delaying collecting can have on your income at a time when you may need it most.

Compared with other forms of income, Social Security benefits have three major advantages. These are:

1. **Cost of Living Adjustments (COLA):** What this means for you is that each year, the Social Security Administration looks at how much the cost of goods and services has increased and adjusts your benefit accordingly. This solves the inflation problem we discussed in Sin #2. The cost of living adjustment is powerful over a long period of time, and is not found in most pensions or annuities. It is another protection against extreme old age.

2. **Guaranteed Income:** Social Security income is about as safe an income as we can find in the world today. Tyler equates the income from Social Security to about the same as holding bonds issued by the U.S. Treasury. The department of Social Security is a branch of the federal government. The federal government is ultimately responsible for the promises made by Social Security. This means that even if the program goes bankrupt in the distant future, the government can always print more money to support the obligations. They have the keys to the printing press. No annuity company or municipality can make that claim.

There is a lot of talk about the viability of the program in the distant future. The concern is whether the Social Security program will be able to meet its obligations. The fact is, by changing benefits to younger workers, lawmakers can solve the problems facing Social Security. It is Tyler's opinion that those in their 50s, 60's, or currently collecting Social Security will have nothing to worry about when the inevitable changes come.

3. **Tax Advantages:** Social Security is tax-favorable income. This means that at most, only 85% of the benefits are taxed as ordinary income. It is often free of state income tax as well, depending on your state of residence. This is more favorable than most other sources of income in retirement, especially annuities. This benefit can save the retiree thousands of dollars per year in tax liabilities; thus, delaying to receive a larger benefit means more tax savings.

These three benefits lead Tyler to recommend that retirees delay collecting their benefits as long as they feel prudent to ensure a larger benefit at a later age. Obviously, delaying benefits is a standard rule of thumb; and as I've demonstrated, rules of thumb can be dangerous. There are several scenarios in which we should consider collecting benefits early. Here are a few:

- Poor health
- Family history of premature death
- Currently in dire financial straits
- Spousal delay of benefits

Until now, we have only discussed collecting benefits if you are single; however, the last reason for collecting early is if your spouse has decided to delay their benefit. This creates the perfect segue to discussing the decision of delaying the benefits of one or more spouse.

In most cases, it is advisable for at least one spouse to delay their benefits as long as possible. As mentioned previously, whichever spouse lives the longest retains the largest benefit of the two. This means that if John delayed his benefit until age 70 and he now receives $2,800 per month and Rebecca only receives half that at $1,400 per month, when John dies Rebecca would receive John's benefit. The larger benefit lives as long as either of the spouses does. Thus, it becomes even more beneficial to allow it to grow as large as possible.

The other advantage of delaying the spouse with the larger benefit is that the spouse with the smaller benefit has the choice of taking their own benefit, or half of their spouses, whichever is larger. So, by having the spouse with the lower benefit collect early and the spouse with the larger benefit collect late, you will not only be able to maximize your benefits, but insure against old age at the same time.

When deciding how spouses should handle collecting Social Security benefits, it is always advisable to seek professional council. Seek out a fee-only CFP® who specializes in retirement planning. They should be able to look at your particular situation and develop a strategy that is right for you.

Solution

The solution to Sin #3 is hopefully apparent by now. In the case of Elmer Braun, his choice to collect his Social Security benefits early led to even larger tax consequences, since he didn't need the money at the time he decided to collect. Delaying Social Security benefits may not be the right move for everybody and your particular situation should be discussed with a professional if there is any question; however, I have met with retirees in their 80s and 90s who have regretted taking their benefit early. I have yet to meet the retiree who regretted taking it late.

Chapter 18
Sin #4: Working with the wrong advisor or No Advisor

"If you can't explain it simply, you don't understand it well enough"
- **Albert Einstein**

Working with the right advisor is the single most important step you can take to ensure retirement success. The mistake made by most retirees is trying to tackle the daunting task of managing their finances themselves or hiring the wrong type of professional. Either of these mistakes can be costly during a time when an error can mean the difference between comfort and distress.

The complexity of investments, Social Security, Medicare, Long-Term Care Insurance, reverse mortgages, and proper asset distribution are challenging even to the professional who works with these subjects daily. The average person who attempts to manage these issues on her own is the equivalent of a criminal who attempts to defend himself because he read To Kill a Mockingbird.

The same is also true for working with the wrong type of advisor. There are various types of financial experts that are all looking for a cut of your investment portfolio or insurance business. However, working with the wrong one is like going to a podiatrist to treat a heart condition. It is vital that the partner you choose to guide you through retirement is an expert in the field who is less concerned with the sale than your well-being.

Their knowledge, experience, and allegiance should provide you with the best chance at financial success in retirement.

These lessons were learned the hard way by most of the people I met on my trip. A good advisor can help their clients avoid most retirement pitfalls. However, the obvious examples of this error were made by both the Grahams of Santa Maria, CA and Marion Ritchie from Henderson, NV. They each are guilty of this sin in a different way.

The Grahams' error was an attempt to manage their retirement funds on their own. They mistakenly assumed that their pension and Social Security would meet their needs, while their investment portfolio would provide for their wants. Peter was confident in his ability to handle the substantial portfolio on his own. Unfortunately, he was wrong. It is not difficult to manage an investment portfolio when the economy is good and markets climbing; it is during the periods of economic crisis and fear that separates the professional from the novice. Peter and Estelle were novices.

The other lesson the couple learned was related to the $40,000 they had given to their granddaughter for college expenses, which turned into a $7,000 error that could have been avoided simply by writing the check to the university directly to cover the education costs. The combined mistakes committed by the Grahams cost them hundreds of thousands of dollars, many times the cost of a good financial advisor. One mistake in retirement can cost the unwitting retiree years, even decades worth of the fee of a good advisor.

Another reason people fail to hire a good financial professional is a lack of trust. Many have a difficult time relinquishing financial decision-making to a third party. It's not difficult to understand why when the headlines are filled with stories of Bernie Madoff, liar loans, Ponzi schemes, and million-dollar executive washrooms. The flagrant abuse of trust that oozed from this industry over the past few years has been nothing short of abysmal. Although it may seem difficult to trust the financial industry in the wake of this mess, most financial professionals are good and decent people who care passionately for their clients. However, to avoid the sharks, follow these simple steps that can help protect you from a con artist in a three-piece suit:

1. **Transparency:** When working with any financial professional, transparency is vital. The ability to check your investment at any time via an independent source such as the Internet can help avoid any shady dealings. The Bernie Madoff scandal demonstrates the importance of transparency. His victims would receive a statement once a year with only a dollar value. There was no mention of where the money was invested and, therefore, the clients had no ability to independently verify the value of their investments. This was all done in the name of confidentiality. It was often explained that Madoff was such a successful investor that if his investments were disclosed, other investors would try to copy his strategy. Do not allow yourself to be "Stonewalled." Even Warren Buffett, perhaps the best investor in history, releases the details of his holdings regularly. If your investment firm is not allowing you to access your investment information on a regular basis, it's time to find a new firm.

2. **Independence:** The best way to ensure that your money is exactly where you expect it to be is by separating the custodian from the advisor. This means that the institution holding your money is independent from the firm or advisor managing the money. Referring again to the Madoff scam, his firm had complete control of and managed the assets. The statements were created by his firm and stated exactly what Madoff wanted them to. There were no checks on this system except

for the Securities and Exchange Commission. By separating the advice from the holder of the funds, you create a scenario where two entities are accountable to each other. It is extremely difficult, if not impossible, to create a Madoff-type scam if the assets are handled this way.

3. **Returns that are too good to be true:** Even the best financial advisors and money managers experience difficult times. When investing, the path to profitable returns is never a straight line. All investors experience periods of good and poor returns. Twenty years of above-market returns should trigger a red flag. There are numerous talented financial professionals that have a long-term history of performing better than average. However, even the best money managers go through slumps. Michael Jordan didn't make every shot he took, but he was still the best in the game. Warren Buffett has had years when his performance fell short of the market. However, it is his overall return that makes him so talented, not a perfect record.

4. **Use Common Sense:** We should all be a little wiser after the experiences in the market, economy, and scandals of the past few years. Let common sense be your guide. If the way your money is being handled doesn't sit well with you, don't be afraid to investigate or make a change. Use your head and focus on independence, and it will be difficult for someone to take advantage of you.

Marion Ritchie also fell victim to Sin #4, but in a different way. Marion made the common mistake of hiring the wrong kind of advisor. She hired a salesman she thought would guide her through the retirement pitfalls, only to be trapped in one he had set for her. Marion's lack of financial knowledge compelled her to take his advice without question. His poor advice led her to refinance her house and use the funds to purchase an annuity

Market Timing Drains Returns

In a remarkable study by DALBAR, a market research firm, you can see the devastation market timing has inflicted on investor returns. The study, updated each year, examines flows into and out of mutual funds for the previous 20 years. Not only did the market timer significantly under-perform both the market itself and the systematic investor, the return was actually negative.

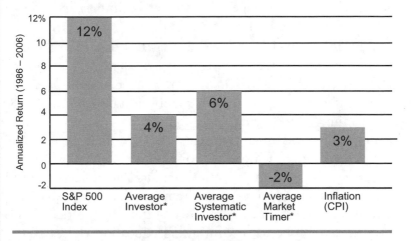

Past performance is no indication of future results.
Measures returns of investors in equity mutual funds.
Source: Bureau of Labor Statistics, DALBAR Quantitative Analysis of Investor Behavior 2007
(dalbarinc.com).

This created layers of fees that generated high commissions for her "advisor." However, when the time came to answer her questions and work with her on an ongoing basis, he was nowhere to be found. Fortunately for Marion, this mistake only cost her about 10% of her net worth. It is often far worse for retirees who make similar errors.

Many individuals who are in business to sell insurance or financial products can and often do call themselves investment advisors. This is the equivalent of a used car dealer calling himself an "Automobile Advisor." It creates tremendous conflicts of interest. A life insurance salesman usually has little or no training in the area of investments, estate planning, or tax planning. Many do have training in their areas of expertise and can be fantastic resources when a financial product is needed; however, salespeople are not retirement planners.

The question becomes, how do we know what type of professional is the right type? The answer is simple: find a fee-only Certified Financial Planner (CFP®).

A CFP® is a financial professional that has met the rigorous qualifications of the CFP® Board of Standards. This means that they have taken classes in the financial planning process, insurance, investments, retirement planning, tax planning, and estate planning. Once they have completed this coursework, which typically takes about two years, they are then given a 10-hour exam covering each of these disciplines. Once the CFP® candidate passes the exam, they must maintain an ethics oath and fulfill three years of experience requirements. Only then are they able to use the CFP® title. And to maintain the certification, they must take 30 hours of continuing education classes every two years to keep up to date with all of the continuous changes in the industry.

The CFP® is the gold standard in the personal finance industry. This individual has the knowledge and experience to help you in all aspects of your finances and can help you focus on your goals and objectives without getting caught up in the day-to-day market minutiae. However, just because an individual is a CFP® doesn't mean they are looking out for your best interest. There are many CFPs® who sell investment products and insurance. This creates a conflict of interest between doing what is right for them or what is a right for their client. This is why it is so important that you find a fee-only advisor.

Financial advisors are paid in three ways: commission, fee-based, or fee-only.

1. **Commission:** A commission-based advisor is a salesman. They give you advice on your finances and encourage you to purchase one of their products to fill your financial need. Their product may be annuities, insurance, mutual funds, etc. The problem with commissioned-based brokers is that they have an incentive to sell you something that may cost you more so that there is higher profit for them. This type of salesman may even sell you a financial product that is completely inappropriate for your financial needs. Handling your finances in this way leaves room for numerous problems.

   Obviously, not all commission-based advisors are scoundrels. Most are honest and hardworking individuals who care deeply for their clients. Unfortunately, it is the compensation structure alone that allows the minority of dishonest individuals to operate and may persuade even the best advisors to put themselves ahead of their clients on occasion or subconsciously cloud their judgment. There is a better way.

2. **Fee-Based:** A fee-based advisor is a broker who earns commissions on the products he sells, but also earns a small fee from you, the client. The purpose of this system is to tie more of the advisor's income to the client. The assumption is that the broker will worry less about the commissions they earn from the products since some of the revenue is coming from the client; thus, keeping the client happy remains paramount. Although it is certainly a step in the right direction, I think we can still see the flaw in this system. The advisor still has an incentive to promote products. Thus, the conflict is not eliminated.

3. **Fee-only:** A fee-only advisor is someone who is paid by the

client alone. They do not receive commissions, kickbacks, or revenue of any kind on any financial product they recommend. 100% of the revenue they generate comes from the client. Thus, the advisor is not beholden to any one product or mutual fund company. They continue to do what is in the best interest of the client to keep the client happy. A happy client continues to pays their fee. There are few conflicts, and the advisor ceases to try to sell the client anything once they are hired.

Solution:

A fee-only CFP® who is looking out for your best interest is optimal. A competent advisor who is not trying to sell you anything will keep you on the right track to ensure that what you have will be there to provide for you throughout your retirement years.

Chapter 19
Sin #5: Paying Too Much in Fees and Expenses

"Beware of little expenses. A small leak will sink a great ship."
- **Benjamin Franklin**

Most retirees concern themselves with large market fluctuations, major economic calamity, or fraud. With good reason, the large, sudden, dramatic loss always seems to be the greatest concern for investors. However, often-overlooked are the consistent, grinding expenses and fees that can gradually eat away at your returns and pin your portfolio down, preventing it from achieving its maximum potential.

Costs matter. It may not seem like much, but when the finance industry pilfers 3% of your return each year, it has a dramatic effect on your income in retirement. John Bogle, the founder of Vanguard and one of the pioneers in low-cost investing said, "With risk constant, high returns are directly associated with low cost."

Frank & Joe

Frank and Joe were best friends in college. They both graduated at the same time and got jobs making roughly the same money. A few years into his career, Frank takes a seminar on investing, the importance of compounding in growing wealth, and the importance of managing fees in your portfolio. He sees Joe at a ball game and tells him all about the seminar, except the part about the fees. Joe gets so excited that he decides to open an IRA at the same time Frank does. They invest in roughly the same asset classes and for 40 years (from the ages of 25-65) they each contribute $5,000 per year. The only difference in the portfolio is that Frank's fees total 1.5% and Joe's fees total 3%.

At 65, these two friends open their statements. Frank's ability to invest wisely, consistently, and with low fees netted him a cool $1,295,282. Joe, despite the fact that he invested wisely and consistently, netted only $878,159. Over $400,000 or one-third of Frank's total savings went into the pockets of the finance industry during the 40-year investing period. A small annual fee may not seem like much until it is compounded over time.

Joe's tale of woe may have little impact on you. I assume that if you are reading this book, you are well past the age of 25 and not concerned about the effect of fees over the next 40 years. Let's, then, look at the case of Ann and Betty.

Ann & Betty

Ann and Betty were both 65 and met each other at a widows' support group. They both wanted to retire and had no intention of remarrying. Despite the $1,000,000 they each had sitting in a savings account, neither had a clue about money and certainly did not know how to generate the income they needed to live. Ann went to a financial seminar and listened to a slick salesman sell her on a financial product he had that would guarantee her $74,549 per year for 25 years. She was so excited, she told Betty with the intention of convincing her to invest as well.

Betty was skeptical. She shopped around and found the same investment vehicle with 1.5% less in commissions and fees. Betty's annual income for the next 25 years was $85,810. She received more than $11,000 per year more than her friend because she was careful to avoid high fees.

The Manning's experienced this phenomenon first hand. Reese and Emma, of Dallas, Texas put their trust in the hands of a friend who they thought was looking out for their best interest. Through the many years they invested with this gentleman, he was investing their nest egg in accounts and vehicles loaded with fees. Those seemingly insignificant fees cost the Manning's over $200,000 in retirement. For those who think fees are insignificant, perhaps the three Mercedes Benz' they are no longer entitled to, 10 trips around the world they could have enjoyed, or 40 trip to Disney World they will never experience with their grandchildren will convince you otherwise.

The Manning's finally got themselves educated about the fees they were being charged, but not before it was too late. They paid a hefty price for their ignorance. It is never too late to get a handle on what you are paying the finance industry. Let's take a look at what fees you may be charged and what is too much.

Loading Fees

Front-End Load – The front-end load is a sales commission that is paid on the front-end of a mutual fund purchase. Front loaded funds can be very painful to a portfolio. It is common to see loads as high as 5.75%. This means that if you were to invest $10,000 in this type of fund, only $9,425 would be invested for you. You would need to have a return of 6.1% just to break even. Sounds like a steep hill to climb.

The front-end load is typically the fee that is paid to your broker for recommending this fund and in theory, providing you with investment advice. I say in theory because I know of many cases where clients are paying these high front-end loads and receiving no advice.

Back-End Load – A back-end load is a load that is incurred if you sell your mutual fund within a certain time frame. These loads are often 5-6% or more if sold in the first year. They typically decline with time before phasing out altogether, usually 3-5 years from the date of purchase.

Annual Expenses

Expense Ratio – This is typically the ongoing expense the fund will charge you for its services. Expense ratios can range anywhere from .05% to 2% or more. Notice that the latter is 40 times more than the former. We now know how dramatic an impact this can have on our return over time. Expense ratios are traditionally taken from dividend payments, so the pain is never felt by the fund owner; there is no monthly check to write, the fund simply pays less at dividend time. Despite the fact that you never receive a bill for your mutual fund expenses, I think we have demonstrated how they can affect your retirement lifestyle.

In the case of Back-End Loaded funds, their expense ratios are typically on the far upper end of the cost spectrum. The reason their loads fade out over time is they want to entice you to stay invested with them for a number of years so they may continue to charge you these tremendously high fees.

Transaction Costs – These are the costs that a broker-dealer will charge you for a transaction. Transaction costs have been in a sharp decline over the last 20 years and are often zero when a certain fund is involved. Be wary of no fee transactions, this usually means the money is being made elsewhere by the brokerage firm. However, many discount brokers now offer stock and ETF (Exchange Traded Funds) trades for as little as $8. This is a far cry from the early brokerage house days when a $100 stock trade was the norm.

Financial Planning Fees – This is simply the cost of a financial plan or is often tied to a comprehensive service including money management. Financial planning fees are a necessary cost, however, some firms will do a financial plan at no cost. They assume that if you implement their recommendations, they will make their money on the insurance and investments sales. Let this Trojan horse into your life very carefully. As we discussed in

Sin #4: Where exactly do their loyalties lie? Paying the planner directly is the best way to ensure they are working for you and only you.

Solutions

We live in a world where cost has a direct relationship to quality. BMW's can be expected to perform better than Chevrolet's, Hagen Daz tastes better than Turkey Hill, and The Cheesecake Factory is better than McDonald's. "You get what you pay for" is a mantra we hear time and again. Although this may be the case on Main Street, the truth on Wall Street is very different.

Studies have shown that the only correlation between fees and returns is an inverse one. Higher fees consistently lead to lower returns. Low fees should not be confused with no fees. As we saw in sin #4, trying to handle your own money usually ends up costing far more than the fee. It is never advisable to avoid one sin by engaging in another.

It is possible to find a fee only CFP® who is concerned about your investment fees as you are. If your financial planner is worth his salt, he will understand the relationship of fees to performance and do everything in his power to keep them as low as possible without sacrificing return.

The use of index funds is the surest way to keep your fees to a minimum and not fret about possible market underperformance. An index fund is a group of stocks that are pre-assigned; they are not actively managed by a fund manager. The index fund tracks an underlying index, like the Dow Jones Industrial Average, and very rarely makes changes to the makeup of the fund. A common example is an S&P 500 fund that tracks (you guessed it) the S&P 500 index. The index is run by a committee and makes changes infrequently, thus, it is not subject to the emotion or whims of an individual whose career is on the line. This can be very beneficial to the investor.

Index funds traditionally have far lower expenses than actively managed mutual funds because they have far less overhead to operate the fund. Index funds usually do not have loads. This is why index funds are so often shunned by full commissioned brokers; there is no commission to be had, thus no income for them. However, fee-only investment advisors are often very receptive to index funds as a large percentage of a portfolio.

Investment fees are unavoidable. In order to have the proper level of diversification, they must be accepted as part of the process. However, all investments are not created equal. Two funds can be exactly the same and have two very different sets of fees. Keeping your fees to a minimum will ensure that you are able to expel every last ounce of juice from your money tree once it begins to bear fruit.

Chapter 20
Sin #6: Trying to Time the Market

"The market timer's Hall of Fame is an empty room."
- Jane Bryant Quinn

It's too tempting to ignore: If I could somehow get a hold of tomorrow's closing stock prices today, I could make a fortune. If I could double my money in that hot biotech stock, like my neighbor did, I could retire early. This is a common mentality not only of retirees, but many investors. Sin #6 is trying to time the market.

We have all heard stories from our friends, neighbors, and families about how they made a killing investing on a hot tip or a great idea. Perhaps you have even experienced this yourself on occasion. The idea of quick money can be alluring. However, if these self-proclaimed market savants are honest with themselves and averaged out their total returns, both wins and losses, it is inevitable that their performance would be far below average market returns. Years of scientific research and a little common sense prove this point.

The average money manager underperforms the market each year. Professionals with years of education, decades of experience, and careers spent doing little else than looking for places to invest money have an abysmal track record when compared to the broad market. If these "experts" have consistently found no success, what chance does your friend, neighbor, or family member have?

Gamblers always seem to recall their victories with remarkable accuracy, while speaking little of their losses. However, it is these losses that tend to more than offset their wins. The truth is, in the world of casino gambling all the lights, glamour, and glitz comes at a price. The more often the player plays, the more likely the casino is to win. The financial industry is the casino; the more often you change your bets, the more money you lose. It's time to swing the odds in your favor.

Bill Lancaster, like most market timers, learned this lesson the hard way. However, unlike most gamblers, Bill was open and forthright about his failures. Bill had a wonderful pension, solid savings, and was poised for a comfortable retirement. His lifestyle was relatively modest, which created no need for him to trade often within his portfolio. He found out quickly what seasoned investors already know - the market cannot be timed with any degree of consistency. This led Bill to a retirement where he is unable to afford even some of the simple comforts he had enjoyed.

Bill, like many retirees, was probably bored. He had this large nest egg and was looking for a way to add some excitement to his retirement. Gambling on the stock market is the choice many retirees make to fill that void. Often drawn in by the allure of a sport that can be won with enough information, they watch financial channels from the couch and trade their hard-earned retirement portfolio speculating on future market moves. Most end up with nothing but a stack of trading receipts to show for their labors.

Market Timing: A Futile Exercise

Academia has proven time and again that the average investor (and even the not-so-average investor) is unsuccessful at trying to time the market. Practical application has confirmed these findings.

The market research firm DALBAR studied market data from

1986-2006 and found that the average investor's return was 4%, the average market timer's return was -2%, and the S&P 500 Index furnished a return of 12%.

As you can see, not only does the market timer perform poorly over this 20-year period, but so does the average investor. The underperformance of almost 8% that the average investor received against the S&P 500 was due to the simple fact that the average investor, even if they do not want or intend to time the market, allow their emotions to dictate their investing decisions.

The problem that continues to haunt investors is the fear of the unknown during a market decline, which eventually leads to selling with the intention of waiting for things to stabilize. Unfortunately, by the time the novice is comfortable reinvesting, they're too late. An SEI study showed what happens when the market turns around after a major correction. If you reinvest at the bottom, you will earn a 32.5% return in the first year and your portfolio will recover its full value, on average, in 1.5 years. But, if you are a week late, your return drops to 24.35% in year one and it will take you 2.5 years to recover. Finally, being three months late drops you to 14.8% and increases the length of your recovery time to three years. Waiting only three short months after the bottom to allow the market to stabilize will cost you a year and a half. That is unacceptable in retirement.

If you sell when the Dow is at 10,000 and falling, will you get back in when the pundits and your neighbors are talking about the end of the world and the Dow hits 8,000? The market is now 20% cheaper, but the average investor is far more afraid. The truth is, the amateur will sell irrationally into a market decline and repurchase when prices are higher. It is this buy high/sell low result that stifles his returns.

If you put $1 in the stock market in 1926, at the end of 2008 you would've had $2,049. But if you missed the 34 best months, you would have had $20.25. So, which months should you be in and which months should you be out?

I think we've made it clear that playing the stock market is an unwise move for the novice, but what about the professional? Surely if I follow the advice of an expert, I am likely to find success. The truth may surprise you.

Researchers at Duke University studied market-timing newsletters, monthly publications that offer predictions on the future movements of stock prices, over a 12-month period and "found strong evidence that as a group, newsletters cannot time the market." In fact, the study showed only 11 of 237 newsletter strategies "could be deemed superior in the long run... that number is less than one would expect by pure chance."

Another study done by Hulbert Financial Digest, a respected source of newsletter information, studied market timers for a 10-year period and found that the S&P 500 gained 18% but none of the market timers equaled that and the average newsletter got only 10% return. This is a pitiful return for a so-called "expert" to whom you're paying your hard-earned money.

The high-profile research firm Morningstar recently released a study that shows just 37 percent of actively managed U.S. stock mutual funds beat their respective Morningstar indexes (bechmarks) after accounting for risk, size and fund style over a three-year period. What is truly amazing is there was no consistency among outperformers. The fund manager who outperformed for one three-year period was actually more likely to underperform the next 3-year period. Why take the chance? You don't need to beat the market; just be the market.

How Could Professionals Underperform?

Most money managers will underperform the market for one simple reason; they are under pressure to perform well each year. The majority of money managers are not investing for the long-term. They do not have the luxury of investing in undervalued assets and waiting for them to become fairly valued. That strategy may take years. They are paid on performance metrics that are evaluated every single quarter.

Money managers are compensated based off of assets under management. A few quarters of poor performance can create a stampede of investors running for the exits. Despite the fact that the investment strategy may be sound when measured over a period of years, the average investor is typically not that patient and will seek a fund that has performed well lately.

Due to their compensation structure, money managers do not want to miss hot trends. So, they will often chase performance and momentum. Think tech stocks in 1999. Who would want to be the money manager explaining to investors why they missed a 30% rise in value because the stocks were overvalued? Investors do not have tolerance or patience for mistakes. There is always another money manager somewhere who took advantage of large positive move, and he or she will see an influx of new money.

This, unfortunately, leads most money managers to make the same mistake that the average investor does: They regularly buy high and sell low. This, along with their usually high costs, leads most active managers to underperform the index on a long-term basis.

Solution:

The solution for Sin #6 is a simple one: When building your portfolio, refer to Sin #2 and build a diversified portfolio that you hold no matter what the news, your favorite market pundits, or your uncle predicts about the market future. Own all asset classes, ride it out and repeat to yourself over and over, "Nobody knows the future."

Nobody has tomorrow's Wall Street Journal. Nobody can say with certainty what will happen to this asset class or that. Don't gamble your money on short-term market swings. Invest in a diversified portfolio designed around your age and risk tolerance, and you will give yourself the best chance at a long and comfortable retirement.

Chapter 21
Sin #7: Lack of Insurance against a major health event

*"When I was younger, I could remember anything, whether
it had happened or not; but my faculties are decaying now and
soon I shall be so I cannot remember any but the things that never
happened. It is sad to go to pieces like this but we all have to do it."*
- **Mark Twain**

Sin #7 may not take as many financial victims in retirement as its six predecessors; however, for those who do fall prey to its ravages, it can cause swift and unmerciful financial devastation.

Insurance, in all its forms, is the most commonly sold financial product in America. Most of us would not think to purchase life insurance or disability insurance if there weren't a salesman in a suit expounding on the heartache of leaving a family destitute due to death or injury.

Insurance is designed to protect us financially. Homeowners insurance cannot prevent our house from burning down, life insurance cannot keep us from dying, and disability insurance cannot ensure our body remains fully functional. These insurances protect our income and assets from catastrophic losses. This financial protection is how we need to frame our insurance decision when we are contemplating a purchase: What exactly am I protecting, and is it prudent to do so?

Never expect your insurance premium to make you money. Similar to gambling at the casino, the odds are always in the house's favor. However, our purchase of insurance should not be seen as a gamble - far from it. It is important to understand that we are paying our insurance premiums with the knowledge and even hope that, most likely, we will never file a claim. However, we are comfortable with this small, affordable, and manageable loss to protect against a large, catastrophic financial loss. There is value in paying a small price to transfer our large risk to the insurance company.

This is how the average pre-retiree needs to view their long-term care (LTC) insurance needs. I imagine it is your desire to pass away quietly, peacefully at home after living an active, healthy life. It may be that way for you. However, what if it's not?

Judith and Tom Kelly made this mistake when they decided against purchasing a LTC policy. Judith explained to me that she didn't see the point in spending $2,500 per year on something they probably would never need. It sounds logical when you are both healthy; unfortunately, that is the same logic that leads so many Americans to die without life insurance and leave their family penniless.

The Kelly's are obviously reaping the misfortunes of the poor decision they sowed years before. Now that Tom needs full-time nursing care, the financial drain has left Judith in dire straits with few options. Although their intention may have been for Judith to take care of Tom if anything were to happen, as is apparent, Tom needs full-time care that would be impossible for Judith to provide, both physically and emotionally. The need for skilled care in our advanced years is almost never planned and is usually out of our control.

The Need for Long-Term Care

Long-term care has become a catch phrase in today's society.

It's a buzzword that many dare not discuss at cocktail parties with aging boomers for fear that they end up standing alone. It's not difficult to understand why; the thought of losing control of your ability to take care of yourself is too much for many to ponder. As difficult as it is to accept, the decision must be faced head-on to avoid a possible financial calamity.

The National Academy of Elder Law Attorneys did a study comparing the risk of financial devastation brought on by long-term care with the risk of financial devastation brought on by a major automobile accident or house fire. According to that study, the rates of incidents were:

House Fire: 1 out of 1,200 [0.08%]

Automobile Accident: 1 out of 240 [0.4%]

Long-Term Care: 1 out of 2 [50%]

The Wall Street Journal writes, "For a couple turning 65, there is a 70% chance that one of them will need long-term care." A study at Harvard University shows that "over 50% of all people entering a care situation are penniless within one year."

We can conclude from the statistics above that for the average 65 year old and their spouse, the risk of needing long-term care, and that need completely wiping them out financially, is about 1 in 3. The thought that a 33% chance of a devastating health event would leave one penniless should create a tremendous fear and outcry for protection. Far more 65-year-olds worry about a 20% temporary market decline. These statistics should make the purchase of long-term care insurance a pre-requisite for a sound retirement plan. However, most people balk at the price and decide they will roll the dice, often with significant consequences.

Let's take a closer look at some LTC statistics:

The national average cost of care for just one year in a nursing home in 2012 is approximately $80,850. In major cities like Boston and New York City, however, one year of LTC can be as high as $150,000.

About 75 percent of all single people and 50 percent of all couples spend their entire savings within one year of entering a nursing home.

92% of all LTC insurance claims are for about three years. 4.5% will need LTC for more than six years.

For every one person receiving LTC in a nursing home, there are four people receiving home health care.

This risk must be addressed. The question for most individuals preparing for retirement is how to best handle it. As with all financial risk, insurance is often the cleanest and simplest way to manage it; however, in the case of long-term care, this may not always be the case. Here are your options.

Self-insure – Self-insuring means that you have the resources to pay for long-term care yourself in the event you need it. The average stay in a long-term care facility is three years. The average cost is $80,000 - $100,000 per year. In order to self-insure, it would make sense that you can comfortably afford a $240,000 - $300,000 expense without impacting your spouse's lifestyle. Obviously, you are retaining the risk that the expense could be far larger if in the rare case that longer care is needed. The expenses could top $500,000+.

A good rule of thumb is to consider self-insuring if you have investable assets of $2 million or more (not including your home). This should provide you with a comfortable enough cushion to absorb this traumatic financial blow. Obviously, this $2 million dollar number may be slightly higher or lower based on your age and expenses. Higher annual expenses may mean a higher self-insure number.

It is important whenever you make a decision about self-insuring that you understand the risk you are retaining. Discuss the pros and cons of self-insuring with a good fee-only planner or long-term care expert that you can pay on an hourly basis. Your particular situation may warrant a deeper discussion than these "rules of thumb" can account for.

Rely on the government – It has become a common mentality with our aging population to assume the government will handle it. Many pre-retirees are under the misconception that Medicare will pay their long-term care costs if and when they arise. The fact is, Medicare only covers acute medical needs, a need that can be treated and cured; it does not cover chronic conditions. This leaves anyone relying on Medicare out of luck if Alzheimer's or Parkinson's were to strike.

The only government program available to help pay long-term care costs is Medicaid. Medicaid is the government-sponsored health care program for low-income individuals. It will cover long-term care costs, but on their terms. Unfortunately, their terms are often difficult to live with.

An individual is only eligible for Medicaid if they have a low level of financial resources. Their guideline for this low level of resource is specific and changes from time to time, but as of this writing in 2011, the spouse of a nursing home resident is limited to one-half of the joint assets up to $109,560. Don't think you can give all your money away to your kids, either; Medicaid eligibility has a 5-year look-back on all gifts. You will be ineligible for some period depending on the size of the resources that were gifted, even if the gift was given a few years back. There can also be hefty gift and income taxes on any gifted money that can make this strategy even less beneficial.

The point is that you will need to burn through most of your resources before you will become Medicaid eligible. This means your spouse could be left to struggle while you are receiving Medicaid benefits - not a desirable position.

The other problem with Medicaid is that only certain facilities will accept it as a form of payment. While you are using your funds to pay for your care, you may get comfortable at the facility or with your home health care worker. Once Medicaid kicks in, that may change. You may be required to change facilities, change home health care workers, or worse, move from home care into a Medicaid approved facility. This is a tremendous loss of control that is overwhelming for many.

Relying on the government is generally not advised unless all other options have been exhausted.

Purchase LTC insurance – This is the most logical path for those who do not have the assets to self-insure. LTC insurance can be expensive by comparison with other insurances. The older you are, the more expensive it becomes. However, it is the insurance that you have the highest probability of actually using, which is why the cost can seem so daunting.

Many who price out long-term care insurance in their 50s are paralyzed by the $4,000 - $5,000/year price tag to cover them and their spouse. Immediately, the mind begins to swim with visions of what that few thousand extra dollars every year could provide; another vacation or two, dinner out almost every week, or a new car every 4-5 years. What is missing during that thought process is what they are protecting against - not the need for care, but the financial devastation to themselves and more importantly, their spouse, that needed care can cause. A few thousand dollars per year will protect you against a significant chance at financial ruin. If your financial advisor told you there was a 1/3 chance that your investments could go to zero and you could protect them all with a small payment of $4,000 per year, would you balk at that decision? Would you put it off?

Yet, many who have spent their lives working, skimping, and saving for the day they could enjoy their money are not willing to lay out a small portion to protect it. If you are older than 45, the time to buy your LTC insurance is today. Don't wait until you are so old that the premiums are unmanageable.

If you are retiring with a net worth of less than $200,000 and are currently older than 60, it is likely the premiums will be unmanageable for you. At this point, your only option is to rely on government assistance if and when the need arises.

Solution:

If you are in your 40s, 50s, or 60s and expect to retire with a net worth of $200,000 to $2,000,000, it makes sense to explore LTC insurance to protect yourself against Sin #7. Statistics show that the lack of this protection for retirees will become more prevalent and could reach epidemic proportions over the next 20 years. The time to prepare for tomorrow is today; repair the roof when the sun is shining.

If it is your plan to self-insure or you cannot afford the annual premium due to low income, spend a little time understanding the financial risks. A small amount of education can go a long way towards making good decisions when tough choices have to be made. If you are not prepared with a LTC policy, be armed with knowledge.

My visit to Garden City, GA was the most heartbreaking of all my stops. The Kellys' problems were more than financial; the universe had seen fit to back Judith into a position where she had to watch the man of her dreams, her best friend for 52 years, deteriorate mentally to a 6-year-old child who does not remember all the good times they had. Although the biggest challenge in life is far from financial, I think the ability for her to remain in her home, to remain tethered to the roots she and Tom laid together, would make this unmanageable situation just a little less burdensome. This is the consequence of a poor financial decision made many years ago when they had the choice. That is the sin that has had the greatest impact on Judith's financial life.

Chapter 22
The 7 Deadly Retirement Sins: A Recap

Sin #1: Retiring too Early/Living Above Your Means

Delaying retirement even a single year can dramatically impact your income level in retirement. Work with a fee-only retirement planner to help you decide exactly how much you will have to live on each year and decide whether that is enough.

Once you do retire, stick to the plan. Do not develop a sense of entitlement. No purchase is worth financial distress in your 80s. Financial peace is invaluable when you've lost your ability to work.

Sin #2: Improper Investment Asset Allocation

Avoid the three major errors in improper asset allocation: over-concentration, inflation, and volatility. Any one of these three portfolio mistakes can lead to a significant loss in the portfolio.

The simple solution is diversification. Never own enough of one asset to make a killing at it or get killed by it. Your portfolio should be made up of stocks, bonds, real estate, commodities, and cash. Regular rebalancing of this portfolio is also important to maintain the proper weighting and improve long-term returns.

Sin #3: Collecting Social Security at the Wrong Time

Social Security is one of the best streams of income you will receive in retirement due to the fact that it is inflation-adjusted, guaranteed by the federal government, and tax efficient. Although each individual situation is different, it is often the case that delaying your Social Security benefit will provide you with a more comfortable lifestyle when you need this income the most. It should be seen as an insurance policy for extreme old age.

Married couples may want the spouse with the larger benefit to delay as long as possible, and the spouse with the smaller benefit to collect as soon as possible.

Sin #4: Working with the Wrong Advisor or No Advisor

The two mistakes most often made in Sin #4 are working with the wrong type of advisor or no advisor at all. It will almost certainly lead to either dramatic underperformance or financial ruin to try to plan your retirement yourself. The right expert should be worth far more than their cost. Look for a fee-only CFP® that can guide you through the storms and help you make the decisions that are best for you. Although it is important to trust your advisor, make sure that you have protections in place to reduce their ability to take advantage of that trust.

Sin #5: Paying too much in fees and expenses

Fees matter! The difference in a high-cost fund or transaction may seem minimal compared to its lower counterpart, but those discrepancies add up to big money over time. Remember, in retirement especially, the returns you are aiming for are not large. A 7-8% return for the average retiree should suffice. However, if 3% in fees are added to the formula, your return suddenly becomes 4-5%. This will absolutely have a dramatic impact on your comfort level in retirement. Get yourself educated on what you're paying in fees and commissions, and find out where there are opportunities for you to save.

Sin #6: Trying to Time the Market

Countless studies and statistics have shown that trying to

outwit the market is a futile task. Professional money managers have had little consistent success, and the average investor has failed miserably. Don't get caught up in the hubris that you know better than most. You don't. When the money you need to live is on the line, the ability to make sound, rational decisions is greatly compromised. Develop a diversified portfolio that is appropriate for your age and risk tolerance and stick with it through good and difficult times. This is the most direct route to financial success in retirement.

Sin #7: Lack of Insurance to Protect Against a Major Health Event

Although many pre- and post-retirees would prefer to bury their head in the sand than face the prospect of long-term care needs, the risk of a major health event causing financial devastation is greater than most people think. If you have less than $2,000,000, it is important that you consider LTC insurance to transfer that risk to the insurance company. Avoid this sin the simple and easy way; purchase a policy that covers the financial risk of LTC needs.

Part IV
What Happens Next?

Chapter 23
Unbelievable

"My Journey Through the Seven Deadly Retirement Sins" was published over nine articles on two relatively small financial websites. Immediately, the series went viral (Internet geek term for "became popular") and I spent much of my time with attorneys negotiating online content deals.

In less than a month, I received a call from the Wall Street Journal hoping for an interview and expose. The journey that began seven months earlier was now gaining so much momentum that I felt overwhelmed. My inbox was flooded with more than 600 emails a day, with questions ranging from various complex retirement topics to people concerned about Mary Dement and the Kelly's. I was touched not only by the positive feedback I had received from those who appreciated the information I was providing, but also by the outpouring of concern for those I had spoken of in the articles.

Only a week after the expose hit newsstands did I receive a call with my first book offer. The request was from an agent who had already contacted publishers that were excited at the chance to publish the book. Tyler and I had always discussed the possibility of a book, but the speed of the demand took me by surprise.

After some discussions with Tyler and exploring a few more agents, we signed with a small firm in Minneapolis that took only a few weeks to sell the idea to a publishing house. All that remained was to write it.

The next seven months were spent working to polish the stories and jump through the hoops of the editing and publishing process. "The 7 Deadly Retirement Sins" hit shelves in April, and the book took off. Its popularity was staggering. The first printing sold out in less than two months, and we reached the top of the best-seller list in less than three months.

The remainder of the year was spent on an exhausting schedule from interviews to book signings. It all seemed surreal, like I was living someone else's life. The reality of our success hit me when I did two nationally televised interviews on Good Morning America and The Today Show in the same week.

These public appearances became the perfect platform to forward my new agenda. It was apparent I was reaching people; the outpouring of correspondence from the public was incredible. I was now receiving over 3,000 emails and letters a day. People had questions, wanted help, and some generously wanted to help those whom I had visited.

There were a total of 33 stops that I made in just over three months, and unfortunately a few of the people I had visited had passed away in the year between the time I visited them and the time I published the book. Their passing was difficult for me. They never got to appreciate how helpful they had been. A fund was established for the remaining 27 sinners (as they became affectionately known), including my Aunt Cindy.

I utilized my newfound platform to promote the fund and plead to the public for their help. Whatever royalties Tyler and I received from the book, 20% each was kept for ourselves while the remainder was divided by 27. Quickly, the "Save the Sinners" fund swelled. It wasn't long before it was time to distribute the money.

Chapter 24
Keeping a Promise

The "Save the Sinners" fund was now sufficiently large enough that preparations were being made on how to best distribute the money. It was an exciting time for me, no doubt the best of my life. After a few meetings with accountants, we were ready. However, before I could begin, there was one stop I had to make.

I arrived in Tinton Falls without warning. As I turned into the driveway, I noticed a large "For Sale" sign on the lawn. I parked the car and rang the doorbell to the old, weather-worn colonial. After no more than a few seconds I saw a shadow appear from behind the stained-glass. Aunt Cindy opened the door, startled, still in her bathrobe and slippers despite the fact it was well after 2:00pm.

"Sam, sweetheart, what are you doing here? Come in, come in. I wish you would have told me you were coming, I would have tidied up the place a bit."

"Hi Aunt Cindy," I said with a smile, leaning forward and giving her a long hug. "I didn't want you to go to any trouble. Besides, it was kind of a spur of the moment thing," I lied.

"Let me put something on, I'm a mess."

"Please don't. It's only me, and I really just came to talk."

Despite my protest, she ducked down the hallway towards her bedroom. She had begun the massive project of packing up her life; brown cardboard boxes were strewn about the house.

"So, what's life like now that you're rich and famous?" Aunt Cindy shouted from her bedroom down the hall.

"Oh stop, I'm just enjoying my 15 minutes. Things are going well, though. I am shopping for a new house." I shouted back.

"That is smart of you," she said on her way back to the living room. "I am glad you are putting all that money to good use. What about Matt, are things still going well with him?"

I had started dating Matt, my new boyfriend, about four months ago. He worked in Tyler's office and we met through the numerous collaborative visits I had there. "Yes, well. Thanks. He is an amazing guy. I am really lucky to have found him."

"Do I hear wedding bells in the future?"

"You sound just like Mom. Maybe, he's definitely marriage material, but it's early yet. We're taking it slow."

"Good for you dear. Get to know the boy first to make sure he's good enough for you."

"What are all these boxes for, you didn't sell the house yet, did you?" I changed the subject.

"No sweetheart, no luck. This real estate market is terrible. I had a few lowball offers, but I can't sell the house your uncle built for so little. I may not have much choice at this point. I don't think I can borrow another dime." She lowered her eyes to avoid mine.

"Good," I said by accident.

"Good!" she exclaimed. "What part of anything I just said was good?"

"It's good you didn't sell the house. I have something for you." I reached into my purse and pulled out a folded piece of paper and handed it to her. She unfolded it and stared in shock. "No, No, I couldn't," she said, choking up. "I can't accept this! You can't give me this!"

"I'm not giving you anything. This is yours. This is your share of our success. There is nothing to refuse."

"I, I don't understand what I did to deserve $407,000?" she

stammered.

"You did everything! This all came from you."

She immediately burst out in an uncontrollable sob and we hugged. She squeezed me tighter than I thought her 84-year-old frame could handle. I softly whispered into her ear, "I love you Aunt Cindy. Thank you for everything!"

"I don't know what to say. This is the kindest, most selfless thing anyone has ever done for me. I feel like this is a dream. You must be an angel sent in answer to my prayers!"

"That's not all. Every month you will receive a check from the royalties of the book, articles, or anything else that comes from 'The 7 Deadly Retirement Sins.' Who knows, maybe they'll even want to do a movie! The point is, you will have regular money coming in for as long as the book sells."

"Unbelievable! Thank you, God!" was all she could muster through her tears.

"I want you to do me two favors, please."

"Anything, just name it."

"I want you to take Uncle Frank's house off the market and I want you to make me that salmon dish again for dinner while I help you unpack these boxes!"

She laughed through her tears. "That is perhaps the two best favors anyone has asked of me. Would you like to come with me to the grocery store?"

"I would love to."

We enjoyed a wonderful day together. I took pleasure from pulling the "For Sale" sign out of the ground on the way out to the store. It was the most satisfying moment of my two-year journey.

We purchased a bottle of Champagne and a nice French Bordeaux to celebrate. We spent the afternoon unpacking, drinking, toasting, eating, and celebrating.

When our evening of frivolity finally came to a close, we said a tearful goodbye and I made my way back through the front door to my car. One down; 26 to go.

Chapter 25
The Time of My Life

All told, the "Save the Sinners" fund totaled just about $11 million when we began cutting checks. This total was a combination of royalties relating to The 7 Deadly Retirement Sins as well as donations that poured in from all over the country. The generosity of the public was overwhelming. This left each household (27 in all) with just over $400,000 each. I wasted no time getting the money into the hands of the people that needed it.

A little over a year and a half after I sat down and spoke with each of these people, they received their check in the mail. Their reactions were as varied as their backgrounds.

Elmer Braun, Monroe, NY

Sadly, my good friend Elmer passed away by the time the book was published. He died in his home peacefully of natural causes. I was fortunate to be able to attend his funeral, as Monroe is not far from my home in Red Bank.

Elmer's family reveled in the stories of his humor, good nature, and love for his family. I even caught another glimpse of that infectious smile of his, which was evident in his youngest grandson, Michael. Elmer will be missed.

Jonathan & Florence Abernathe, Taylor, MI

Jonathan and Florence were both surprised and excited by the delivery of their check. They had seen me on television and read the book numerous times. They were so proud to be involved with such a worthwhile project that they gave my book to all their friends and family for Christmas.

A few days after the delivery of their check, I received a call from Jon. He told me how much he appreciated the gesture, and that he would like to pay it forward. He informed me that they had used about $60,000 of the money to pay a few outstanding medical bills and would like to donate the rest to Judith and Tom Kelly. In Jon's words, "Sure, we made some mistakes, but what happened to us was nothing compared to what happened to Judith. We've discussed it for the past few days, and would really like to do this for her."

My attempts to dissuade him were futile, they had already made the donation. The previous day, the "Save the Sinners" fund received a check for $347,000 with a note asking that it be given to the Kelly's and the donor remain anonymous.

Jonathan and Florence still live a comfortable life in Michigan. They use their share of the annual royalties to visit their family and travel. I speak with them regularly and have seen them recently when they surprised me at a local book signing. They were received as celebrities by the crowd and spent the afternoon signing countless books.

Julio & Maria Espinoza, Florence, OR

Julio & Maria Espinoza were not so fortunate to have the ability to donate their funds back. Immediately after they received their check, Maria called me in tears to thank me for the generous gift. "You have no idea what this means to us," Maria gushed. She went on to tell me how her six-year old granddaughter, Anna, was diagnosed with a rare form of Leukemia. Anna would be undergoing treatment in the next few weeks and Julio was away, helping their son make preparations for the upcoming ordeal. Maria could not attend the treatment as they could not both afford to travel.

Maria wept as she spoke about how this new money would allow them to spend time with their granddaughter throughout this difficult time. She was grateful and touched.

Peter & Estelle Graham, Santa Maria, CA

Estelle received the check while Peter was out one day. Before Peter came home and became aware of their newfound fortune, Estelle had called two people. One was a real estate agent about buying something that would, as she put it, "get us out of this dump!" The other call was to a financial planner. Apparently, Peter and Estelle learned a lot from my book and were not going to make the same mistake twice.

The last I heard, Peter and Estelle were doing wonderfully. They bought a house in their old neighborhood of Santa Maria and were getting along much better (according to a conversation I had with Estelle recently). Any resentment or blame they had towards one another seemed to have lifted with their windfall. They were even able to spend more time with friends who they hadn't seen in some time.

Mary Dement, San Diego, CA

Mary received her check with great joy and enthusiasm. I spent almost an hour on the phone with her as she tried adamantly (without success) to return the money, which eventually allowed Mary to keep and maintain her condo.

I see Mary regularly. We make it a point to get together twice a year for "girls' nights," as she calls them. Unfortunately, Mary's health has deteriorated, so I am happy to make the trip to visit her. She cooks me a large dinner (always served on the finest china) and we drink martinis on the patio. It has become a tradition, and I am not sure who looks forward to the trips more. She has also been a good friend with helpful advice about life and love. I am pleased to see the strain of financial pressure lifted off her shoulders. If you think she was feisty before, you should see her today!

Marion Ritchie, Henderson, NV

Marion Ritchie was another one of my friends who had passed away before the book was published. Apparently, during my visit with Marion, we were both unaware that she had an inoperable brain tumor. It seems apparent to me now that her forgetfulness was more than just old age. Marion passed away the winter before the book came out. She never saw her story in print.

I was heartbroken when I heard the news. Marion struck me as a kind and gentle soul who would give you the shirt off her back. Even though we only had the one meeting, her influence on my life was profound and the lessons she taught will not soon be forgotten.

Reese & Emma Manning, Dallas, TX.

Reese called me immediately to thank me but told me that he and Emma could not accept the gift. Despite my best attempts, Reese was adamant. The Manning's had read my book and heard the stories of those who had suffered great losses due to silly mistakes. With a successful business shooting them regular income, they did not consider themselves in the same category. I mentioned to Reese about what the Abernathe's had done, and Reese and Emma both agreed they would like to do the same. They donated the money to the fund for the Kelly's.

The case of Reese and Emma was never a desperate one; however, their generosity is still greatly admired. It is a rare and unselfish person who could refuse a check for over $400,000.

Bill Lancaster, Deerfield Beach, FL

It would be a lie to say I was unconcerned about handing a check over to Bill for $407,000. I could see it vanish in the flash of the roulette ball after a few trips to Vegas. This was unsettling, and Tyler and I spent some time trying to figure out a solution to the problem.

After some discussion, we decided on a plan that would provide Bill with the income he needed without the temptation to gamble the money. Tyler sent Bill the paperwork for a low-cost fixed annuity that would provide Bill with a substantial guaranteed income for the rest of his life. Although there was an inflation concern, given his age, this seemed like the most appropriate solution. This rather large stream of income, along with his share of the ongoing royalties, would ensure he could live out his days in a comfortable manner. He could fish, travel, and spend more time with friends.

I received a call from Bill immediately after he received the annuity and he was practically speechless. The rock of a man actually began to choke up. Bill was perhaps more appreciative of his newfound financial success than any retiree I'd heard from since Aunt Cindy. I was stunned by his overwhelming gratitude.

Judith & Tom Kelly, Garden City, GA

It was a Tuesday afternoon when I received the call from Judith. Her voice was barely audible, "Sam. Sam. What is this check all about?"

"Did you read the letter I sent? That is your share of the royalties and donations we have received so far."

"I don't understand. Is this money ours?"

"It is. You will also receive your share of all the future royalties in a monthly check."

"Why?"

"Why? Why? Judith, you helped me create this book. People heard your story and wanted to help. You have suffered far too much in the past few years. You should not have to worry about your finances. That's why!"

She began to cry uncontrollably. "Oh thank you! Thank you so much! Thank you, Jesus!"

All told, the Kelly's received a check for just over $1.1 million. This was more than enough money to support Tom and allow Judith to remain in her house.

The suffering that Judith was experiencing was more than financial. She had been her husband's rock, despite the emotional toll it has taken on her. It was a pleasure to be able to help this woman, even if only financially, who was paying far too high a price for a misstep years ago.

Thomas and Latesha Gibson, Holly Springs, N.C.

I received a call from Latesha right after she and Thomas had received their check. She was so excited to see me on her favorite morning talk show. She told all her friends to go out and buy my book.

She was overcome with joy when she received her share of the funds. They were prepping the house for sale when the check arrived. I realized the magnitude of what the gift meant to them; they would never have to leave their beloved home. I joked that I would be coming down to visit for weeks at a time. Latesha laughed, and it lightened the mood.

She and Thomas were so touched by the generosity of those who helped them, that they have been spending much of their time volunteering with a teen outreach program. They felt the desire to give back for the kindness that had been shown them.

Chapter 26
The End of a Long Journey

It has been over two years since I received that fateful phone call from my mother, asking me to check in on my Aunt Cindy. This relatively short period of time has changed me profoundly. It's not the financial success or the 15 minutes of fame, but my perspective, the rose-colored glasses through which I now see the world. Hopefully, this book, the people in it, and its attempt to share that journey will furnish you with a small measure of that perspective.

Despite our best efforts to avoid financial challenges in retirement, we are sometimes faced with a path that splits before us. We must decide which direction to go if we are to move forward. The common thread underlying all the mistakes outlined in this book is the decision based on emotion. These impassioned choices can destroy your retirement dreams and ruin the best-laid plans.

Investors teem with emotion when the market is volatile, greedy when the market is high, fearful when it's low. They are emotional when the decision to purchase a long-term care policy is delayed, because they often cannot face the prospect of the conversation. It is emotion that compels many to take Social Security benefits immediately when they become available, because the thought of the government winning is too much to bear. Finally, our emotions tie us to the stock we inherited because "Dad owned it for decades."

I am not condemning emotions. They allow us to feel,

laugh, give, and love. They are the symbol of our humanity. However, emotions wrapped in financial decisions consistently lead to poor ones.

Each of the retirees involved with this project were given a second chance. They were fortunate enough to get a "do-over" in an often cold, harsh, and unforgiving world. Unfortunately, there is little chance you will receive a similar opportunity. You only have one crack at retirement. It is incumbent upon you to get it right the first time.

As the ghost of Christmas Future provided for Ebenezer Scrooge, these stories are a glimpse into a possible future for you. Fortunately, your future is not yet written. Your life, and your retirement, is yours to make whatever you desire. Keep the lessons of these sinners and The 7 Deadly Retirement Sins as you take your journey. I promise you, they will serve you well during a time when even one mistake is too many.

Final Note: Enriching Your Life

*My favorite things in life don't cost any money. It's really clear
that the most precious resource we all have is time.*
- Steve Jobs

Retirement is not about money. Retirement is about freedom,
exploration, and your ability to enrich your life, as well as the
lives of those around you. However, money is vital much the
same way water is vital to a human being. You would not last
long without water; nevertheless, I doubt if anyone would define
their life by the quantity of water they drink. Money, like water,
is a necessary resource that provides us with the capability to
achieve our dreams and enrich our lives.

As you progress towards and through your retirement, it is
my hope this concept remains with you. At Zynergy Retirement
Planning, we offer several resources and programs—many of which
are at no cost to you—to help you maximize your retirement and
enrich your life. Visit us at www.zynergyretirement.com to sign
up for our digital magazine, The Impractical Retiree, or "like" us
on Facebook. We provide these free resources to help you get the
most out of your time in retirement. They include useful topics,
such as maximizing your time with grandchildren; local theater
and arts; community events; and, food and wine.

Time is, without a doubt, our most precious resource.
Retirement is the stage in life when this resource is plentiful and
your own. Make it count. Make your retirement extraordinary.
Enrich your life!

About the Author

Ryan Zacharczyk, CFP®, MBA is President of Zynergy Retirement Planning, LLC, a financial planning firm specializing in working with mature adults 50 years old and above.

For almost a decade, Ryan worked as a financial trader for Bear Hunter, a Manhattan specialist firm on the New York Stock Exchange and the American Stock Exchange.

Ryan is a frequent speaker at several corporations and organizations as well as at Active Adult Communities, Senior Groups, and Chambers of Commerce. Topics include "Retirement Planning for Any Age", "Living Off Your Assets", and "Social Security & Medicare".

In addition, Ryan has written numerous articles related to retirement and financial planning. He is the personal finance writer for both "Dummies.com" and "Currents" magazine.

Ryan is on the Executive Board of Directors of the Eastern Monmouth Area Chamber of Commerce where he is the vice-chairman.

Mr. Zacharczyk holds a Certified Financial Planner™ designation, Certified Retirement Planning Counselor designation, and Accredited Wealth Manager Advisor.

Ryan received two degrees from the University of Connecticut, where he was captain of their Division I swim team. His Bachelors of Science is in Business, while his Bachelors of Arts is in Communications. Ryan has also received his MBA in finance from Monmouth University.

Ryan lives in Oceanport, NJ.

Peter

- can he go to 2 food pantrys per mo.
- help w. utilities
- food stamps
- train & bus pass
- medicaid
- meet w. Sue Their
- call DDD - possible fu Pete?